DAD, I WROTE!

THE VEIL

BEVERLY BRAXTON

authorHOUSE

AuthorHouse™
1663 Liberty Drive
Bloomington, IN 47403
www.authorhouse.com
Phone: 1 (800) 839-8640

Published by AuthorHouse 08/09/2018

ISBN: 978-1-5462-5501-7 (sc)
ISBN: 978-1-5462-5499-7 (hc)
ISBN: 978-1-5462-5500-0 (e)

Library of Congress Control Number: 2018909589

Print information available on the last page.

CONTENTS

PREFACE

The transformation from Joan to Charlotte was not the only struggle Charlotte had. She had to struggle to maintain herself as her memory began to unfold and God gave her the full insight on where she came from, who was with her, and how the atmosphere and connection to others were designed.

God allowed Charlotte to be born in the Caribbean, and not in the United States, where her brother was born.

God allowed Charlotte to be born to Careen and Heath. Although Heath knew of her brother, she was the only one after coming to the new world who knew there was a brother.

God did not allow Heath to continue in her life as an earthly guidance. His mission was complete when he put her on the airplane to bring rest to Careen's wandering spirit. Her mission too was complete; she had brought Charlotte to the United States, and now He would perform His purpose by showing them His greatness from the ends of the earth. Luke 12:7 promises, "Indeed, the very hairs of your head are all numbered."

PSALM 139:1-18

You have searched me, Lord,
  and you know me.
You know when I sit and when I rise;
  you perceive my thoughts from afar.
You discern my going out and my lying down;
  you are familiar with all my ways.
Before a word is on my tongue
  you, Lord, know it completely.
You hem me in behind and before,
  and you lay your hand upon me.
Such knowledge is too wonderful for me,
  too lofty for me to attain.

Where can I go from your spirit?
  Where can I flee from your presence?
If I go up to the heavens you are there;
  if I make my bed in the depths, you are there.
If I rise on the wings of the dawn,
  if I settle on the far side of the sea,
even there your hand will guide me,
  your right hand will hold me fast.
If I say, "Surely the darkness will hide me
  and the night become night around me,"
even the darkness will not be dark to you;
  the night will shine like the day,
  for darkness is as light to you.

For you created my inmost being;
>   you knit me together in my mother's womb.
I praise you because I am fearfully and wonderfully made;
>   your works are wonderful,
>   I know that full well.
My frame was not hidden from you
>   when I was made in the secret place,
>   when I was woven together in the depths of the earth.
Your eyes saw my unformed body;
>   all the days ordained for me were written in your book
>   before one of them came to be.
How precious to me are your thoughts, God!
>   How vast is the sum of them!
Were I to count them,
>   they would outnumber the grains of sand—
>   when I awake, I am still with you.

CHAPTER 1

*C*areen

The veil of life that embodies us and allows us to reach and seek beyond our horizon conceals the dreams that plague our spirits through unrest. In so doing, we venture onto paths unknown that lead us from the protection of God's will. But when we place our unrest into the hands of Jesus, God's will is brought into view, revealing a road map that directs each individual to contribute to the fulfilling of God's purpose. Wynona whispered under her breath on day as memories flood her mind of the wasted and foolish path that her careen and Julia decide to explore their journey to freedom and happiness.

Domesticity was the resilient cord woven through generations of Jamaican families in the West Indies community where Careen was born and raised. Without question, domestic and farm labor were the certain futures most children grew into, and the heritage was passed on to their children. Careen, however, was different. From a very early age, she was a wanderer and a dreamer who saw a different future for herself. She was restless, and in her spirit she was being driven. Months had passed and Wynona and Julia happened across each other they stood for a moment and began talking about their teenage path, Julia said this domestic life is back breaking, but life is sweet in this land call Jamaica, no matter how I travel Jamaica is home. you hear from careen she made up her mind she was out, not even little cold water she splash behind her, like she know where she was going.

Unsure of her path, she explored every challenge that appeared to have an answer to her restlessness. Domestic chores, whether working inside their home or outside on their farm, were too mundane, too routine for Careen to consider as her expected future. She simply couldn't accept the thought. She didn't understand why she felt different from her ten siblings.

Careen was innovative; she had dreams and wanted to make them a reality. She longed for something more, something exciting to reach for, a career out in the world beyond the boundaries of her Jamaican heritage. That longing grew as she grew. Careen dreamed that she would one day move far from familiarity to a world beyond her present knowledge and understanding. From deep within her, she felt called away. Careen, the youngest child, had inherited her mother's beauty and shapeliness; she had a face you looked at twice. Careen's physique attracted more attention than she wanted from men, yet she was level headed. Wish her the best, Wynona said maybe she is a model or got into the movie business.

Careen and her siblings were raised in a loving, happy, and very busy two-parent home. Their house was small for thirteen people—two parents raising eleven children—but their home was well cared for. Her parents and siblings were dedicated to the daily chores that kept their home functioning well and flourishing. Careen's siblings grew to love and care for their home as an invaluable commodity and felt as though they lived in a mansion.

Daily chores on their farm were orchestrated by Careen's parents, not only in quest of training their children for their own future successes but also to keep the passel of children occupied and entertained. The repetitive chores of cooking, baking, laundering, and tending to the gardening and animals were distributed among the family members, except Careen. She was often overlooked when chores were assigned, because her sisters saw her as a precious button and did not want to load the burden of housework on her, so she had the freedom to roam and dream. How she got through so fast its as if something open a path for her and she slip in, well said Julia we will cross path my visa won't expire without a visit in the states once or twice a year at least she left something behind if not cold water

Careen was a bundle of joy, and her beauty deterred any harsh reprimand from her sisters, who protected her from their parents' stern upbringing. As she watched the never-ending cycle of domestic life, she longed in her heart with determination for something completely different for her future. Some of her siblings saw her as determined and headstrong in the path she had chosen as her exit from a nonproductive life

The family was not a churchgoing family. Although Careen's siblings gravitated toward different denominations for worshipping the Lord, Careen did not feel led to adopt any worship denomination. She never prayed or talked about God. She did not have a spiritual mind toward God. She did not want to entertain the idea that there is a God and that we are on this earth to fulfill and complete His wishes. Careen had a goal and believed with determination and self-will that she should set out to search for her own destiny.

Like most others in their community, Careen's father, uncles, and brother were carpenters and masons. They helped build many of the brick buildings that stand in downtown Kingston. Grandfather Charles Sylvester humpry helped build the oldest boys' school in Jamaica. When construction and masonry work were slow, Careen's family depended on farming and livestock as their source of sustenance and income. They grew much of their own food and raised their own livestock, including chickens, goats, cows, and pigs. Their heritage derived from the richness of the earth and the labor of their hands. Only necessities that were not homegrown were bought from the local market, including butter, cornmeal, flour, and sugar. Julia if we stand here and reminiscing any longer we go need a bed but memba the cook outs the food at her parents house we never hungry, look ya call me. now me feel like careen fly fly away when me look pan the work.

These thoughts flowed through Careen's mind while she watched the steady regimen of work from a discerning and contemplative distance. There were fruits and vegetables to pick, goats and cows to milk, and eggs to gather. The work was rewarding but sometimes came with its challenges. Careen would often look back on her childhood with a different view of some of its tensions. For example, a chicken perhaps wanted to brood on her eggs to produce hatchlings, yet the family wanted those eggs for breakfast, leading to a rowdy disagreement between fowl and egg gatherers.

The family supplied both brown and white eggs from their chicken coop; Careen was not particular about the flavor. Just as she could not distinguish their chickens' brown eggs from the white eggs by taste, she found a distinguishable difference in the home of the family where she worked. Her employers purchased all their supplies from the market or the corner store and were not liberal with giving or sharing their food. She wanted to feel as her employers felt at the independence of not relying on the farm except to buy from the market.

Home and farm life was very different. Their products came from the ground or from selecting a goat, chicken, or pig for the table. Careen's thoughts fluttered through her childhood. The family grew vines of clustered tomatoes, yellow and white yams, and Irish and sweet potatoes. White yams were Careen's favorite; the yellow was best in pumpkin soup with dasheen, a root vegetable more commonly known as taro. Careen would sit and watch as her sisters cut potatoes and yams from vines and tossed them into a basket to be carried to the kitchen. Green peas grew on vines that looked like little trees, with many limbs that were weak and lay close to the earth. Careen watched as her sisters hulled them and filled their aprons or a basin with fresh green peas. Those that dropped would be watered by rain, and after a time, the first two little leaves would sprout. Not long after, a vine would begin to grow. Thus, the repetitive cycle of life continued from the earth as well as in Careen's home and on their farm.

Banana trees grew in clusters, and each produced six to twelve bunches of green bananas. Plantains, members of the banana family, were cut down and stored in a dark, cool place and checked every couple of days to see if they had turned yellow and were ripe. Unlike many farmers, Careen's family didn't spray anything on their fruits, bananas, and plantains to enhance coloring. Their bananas and other fruits were allowed to naturally ripen to their original colors, which made the taste exquisite in their natural juices.

Careen would sit and watch as her sisters cut potatoes and yams from vines and toss them into a basket to be carried to the kitchen. She watched as her sisters and brothers became land lovers, plowing the land to reproduce. When the rain did not fall, they would carry several buckets of water to water the ground, repeating this process until rain fell. Some of the neighbors would come and help in cultivating the land.

Once this love of the land had brought forth large cabbage, healthy yams, and potatoes, a feast was in order, and a cow or large goat would be sacrificed. Most people in Jamaica did not own a refrigerator; food was shared with neighbors. A water bucket would hold several lemons or limes with sugar for the lemonade drink, and the families would gather. There were many children who played games like ring-around-the-rosy and sang those rhythmic games like go dunn a manuel road gal and boy to go bruck rock stone. If you slow you get your finger mash, so don't think, nor listen to the music long. The older male siblings were in charge of the music, while the uncles and dads played dominoes. These gatherings always lasted until early morning. Therefore her grandfather always recommended having a feast on Friday or Saturday. Even thou they use to mash me finger said Sharon the music was nice, as she snap her finger and move from side to side, because of uncle Charles sharon couldn't get up to dance like she feel it so she dance in her mind and the rock tell the rest.

Careen watched all the repetitive activity and could not imagine following in the footsteps of her parents and siblings. She dreamed of a world beyond their land and home—and beyond Jamaica. She watched as her siblings gathered their homegrown cocoa seeds and prepared them on Saturday evening. They grated the seeds and then put them in the mortar, a stone basin where seeds were mashed to powder. The powdered chocolate was used to make fresh hot chocolate. This was a special treat for Sunday mornings but, like the other bounty of their land, not so special to Careen that it would hold her heart to a future of farming or domestic work. She was decisive and determined.

One of the desires of Careen's heart was to be married and have children. She wanted to have the husband–wife unity she saw her parents portray in her home, and she went about seeking for that relationship without God or prayer. After high school she would wander off with friends she believed would lead her to where she would be able to make her dreams a reality. She was eighteen and did not talk with just any young man. He had to be ambitious and have a will to seek higher things from life.

She met a young man who had just enrolled to become a police officer, and they began dating. But their dating was short-lived. He moved too slow for Careen's expectation. He talked of being a constable in the force; his thoughts were not helping her to travel. Careen yearned for fulfillment and did not find it with the officer. It was a disappointment for her. Although they dated for a while. She walked away with the after effect of self-will. Nothing can interfere with the will of God. If they had married,

God's will would have been interfered with. He was a police officer with a drive to achieve the highest rank in his profession. So what you think Wynona careen had a good man in Phillip she would have had the good life she wanted, he would have allowed her to travel, yes said Wynona but seeing and knowing more about this journey she had to follow her path even if without the Lord. So you really believe she was on this path without the Lord.

Careen became pregnant by the officer while they dated. After she had given birth to their son, she handed him his child and moved on; the relationship was over. She wanted to be free to entertain her thoughts and longings. She had to move back home until her next decision and she would not be accepted with a baby. Besides, a baby would slow her pace, and she felt she was just beginning to gain her place and be in control of herself.

She started looking for jobs. At the time the only jobs available were domestic work: taking care of children, cooking, and housecleaning. In doing this she was able to once again move from her parents' home. She found a room on her days off and began her adventures.

Careen was disappointed about the birth of her son out of wedlock, as she did not want to have children before being a wife and having a husband. She desired to be married. She continued her adventures for a change from the mundane routine of her home life, but what she found in town was the tireless familiar conversations about finding a husband and making the land fruitful. Careen was almost certain that such thoughts were not able to fulfill her yearnings. Yet she continued to keep herself in their company; they had the excitement she was looking and the connections she was interested in, but their conversation was not of interest to her Those were the common hopes of the peers, and she felt a desire to be somewhere besides her homeland. She did not know where, but she knew she had to keep searching for a path to escape. Still, despite her disappointment with her peers' conversation, she refused to consult with the Lord as to her next step.

She ventured out further, getting together with her friends when the ships came into dock at the wharf for a week or a month with the servicemen coming from war. Careen was among the several young females waiting for the soldiers to unload onto the dock. She found herself entertaining one of the sailors for the duration of the ship's docking at the wharf. Her goal was to travel from her homeland. Her thoughts were so focused on finding passage that she did not consider that this adventure might impede her path. When the ship set sail and left port three months later, she was left with only a memory. And when the ship left the dock the sailor had left his prize behind with no information, neither roots nor branch. Well, look at the dangers we endured we could have been dead several times, if the Lord was not in the plan, maybe it wasn't His divine plan, but, he was there, said Wynona

When her daughter was born nine months later, and with no history of the baby's father, Careen had to face responsibility with a gift too precious and beautiful to walk away from, She could not give this child to anyone; the connection had been broken. Careen found herself spending days and nights at the hospital. Her baby had been born with sickle cell anemia. One of her neighbors, Valarie Henry who felt Careen's turmoil and sadness, began staying with her at the hospital and when it was time to register the baby, the neighbor said, "Give her my name." So Careen's baby left the hospital with a first, middle, and last name. In Jamaica, when you have a child, it should carry the last name of the father, and she became Careen's adventure, her little Caucasian baby. Although this slowed her adventurous spirit, spending time at home with her new baby only inspired her thoughts even more to venture out.

After her baby was stable, she began visiting her family, mainly her sisters and nieces. She brought the baby, and after recovering from her daughter's birth and finding acceptance from her family, she had gained the confidence to leave her baby with her sisters and nieces until she came back from new adventures. She still had a yearning deep within her that needed to be filled. As they began to stand by her side, she had gained the confidence to leave her sickly baby daughter in their care and try to fulfill the yearning deep within her. Yes, she was restless, but, what burden she was carrying to pass up Phillip,

> It is through our everyday journey in life
> That we give God the highest praise.
> But if we do not know the creator of
> Life, we then stumble through this world.

From the overabundance of foods they grew, each sibling brought the fruit of their labor to the family table. Mealtimes were a delight, with each family member's perfected specialty brought to the large dining table. Compliments went out for the most delicious food. Meals were like a catered service, offering an array of savory dishes, including goat marinated in thyme, scallions, black pepper, and the finest Jamaican curry; or escovitch fish, which is marinated with a peppery vinegar-based dressing and served smothered with sautéed onions, fried plantains, bami, Jamaican gangue peas, and rice. And there was fresh fruit. But despite the delicious reaping and the camaraderie of family working, playing, and enjoying life together, Careen wanted more. She wanted something different.

As different as each sibling was from the others, everyone but Careen seemed content with the work of planting, harvesting, and preparing garden foods and tree fruit. They did not question that this way of life was their future. While her siblings worked diligently on the family farm and in their home, Careen freely strayed across the many acres they owned. While she enjoyed the pastured cows and goats, the thought of raising the animals, growing her own food, and keeping a home had not taken root in her as it had in her siblings and most Jamaican communities. Careen saw the world around her differently.

Although she could not fully grasp its complete intentions, the big family would gather in their yard after a long day's work and tell stories of the family history and old folktales. Careen listened, but the older she got, the more distant her thoughts wandered about what the world at large held for her. Like the friends she visited, Careen's sisters limited their hopes of the future to practical improvements. She struggled with the discomfort of unrest and envisioned for herself a future in a land unknown to her and her siblings. One thing I can say Careen left me with the joy of working and earning my own money listening to her about her freedom give me the idea I should try this work and see how independent I feel.

One day when Careen was a teen, she ambled through the pasture and wandered off the property and into town as she sometimes do. There she sought companionship and adventure with other girls. She listened to and grasped their ideas that fit her will and desire for fun, but what exactly was it?

Careen was disappointed in most of the conversation she heard.

Her peers were not trying to venture out and talked about unproductive adventures that would limit their travels. Careen wanted to be married but to a man with an adventurous spirit, wanting more than what was presented to him. She desired to be married and then have her children. She wanted to be able to travel between the land that would give her the freedom to live her dreams and the country that she thought would never set her free. She did not want to be stationary; she did not want to follow the path of her ancestors.

Careen continued her search for a change from her mundane home life, but what she found in town was the tireless familiar conversations about finding a husband and making the land fruitful. She was almost certain that such thoughts would not fulfill her yearnings. Those were the common hopes of the peers that she knew, and she wasn't impressed. They found wonder in the idea of flushing toilets, lights that could be turned on from a switch, and hired help to milk the goats and cows, feed the chickens, and gather eggs. These were the hopes and dreams of Careen's siblings and neighboring peers. You know Wynona Careen wasn't dreaming you know she was doing something about her dreams, we was too busy trying to get the crumbs, but wait they, me get me visa, man, me can travel any time, and you get Rodney and his eight pickney. No a ten two ano fe him.

Yet that was only a dream for them. Their thoughts were centered on the way of life they had always known. And as history foretold, they would sow those domestic seeds with contentment into the next generation. Deep inside, Careen knew she had been created for a different purpose than what had bound her family and communities for centuries. Though she was uncertain what occupation she would one day pursue or where dreaming and determination might take her, she allowed the energy of restlessness to propel herself to leave the legacy of domesticity behind and not look back.

Careen continued leaving her baby with her sisters as often as they would watch the pretty delicate baby. Careen was innovative and had dreams and wanted to make her dreams a reality. She was restless in her spirit. Feeling driven yet unsure of her path, she explored every challenge that seemed to offer an answer to her restlessness. Yet she refused to consult with the Lord as to her next step.

Careen had many promising qualities. She was a beautiful person who decided that the lifestyle that enveloped her family was not sufficient to calm her restlessness. She had inherited her mother's beauty, which drew more attention than she wanted from men, yet she was levelheaded when she communicated with boys. She chose and spoke with men who had a title or appeared to be going somewhere. Her first boyfriend was a police officer who became a constable. Careen was seeking answers outside the will of God.

But the question is Where does God want me to go, and what does God want me to do?

Jeremiah 45:5 (NKJV) says,

> "And do you seek great things for yourself? Do not seek them; for behold I will bring adversity on all flesh," says the Lord. "But I will give your life to you as a prize in all places, wherever you go."

Careen had an appointment without information. This made her restless and driven. Therefore she found herself running here and there, seeking an answer to her appointment, but she still did not take the time to converse with God as to why this restless spirit was upon her.

As she traveled through paths of promises, she met a man called Heath who had a promising future. He was an in-house resident as a schoolmaster, being trained as a headmaster for the school he graduated from. He was also seeking for a path. Careen and Heath became attracted to each other. He would come to Careen's parents' home when she was visiting with her parents on her days off from work, but like most parents, they knew when their daughter was bringing home a future son-in-law. And they did not bond with Heath; therefore they discouraged Careen from dating him. However, Careen continued meeting Heath in discreet places without drawing her parents' attention. But when Careen began gaining weight, her parents, being old-fashioned, knew Careen had gotten herself pregnant. They relented and allowed her to manage her life as she had chosen for herself. Careen sister grace had mention to careen that she was not going to be married to heath because she heard he was only testing the waters these words only made Careens' will stronger towards pursuing Heath.

In July 1955 Careen was still getting to learn of Heath's world. She found that she was not the only one he was dating, and her pregnancy was his fourth. Careen was disappointed to learn about his love interests, who were very adventurous and also exploring his challenges. He had met them and fathered many children with like-minded explorers. Heath was a freethinker and had no intentions of becoming committed to any one woman. There she is careen said to herself as she watch heath coming from her door and he passed his hand over her belly. He smiled close to her hair then walked away.

Birth control was not available in the early 1950s, and women were getting pregnant in hopes the man would marry them and start a family. But Heath had a variety of women, and most of them were pregnant and giving birth in succession. This interfered with his intentions of being adventurous when they began asking for monetary gifts. As a student he had little to offer; after giving birth, his explorers quickly realized that his Idris Elba physique was all he had to offer. They quickly moved on in hopes of finding the way of escape. Heath was like the children of Israel circling Mount Sinai without an exit.

During this time Heath wandered into a gate that had a gatekeeper. This gatekeeper found out his daughter was pregnant, and Heath was responsible. He challenged Heath, who had no choice but to become a husband. At this time Careen was slowly domesticating Heath, but now he had to get married. When Careen found out about the arrangement, being of a polytheistic religion, she was very angry. Her presumed relationship was over. She would not be a wife, and she had another child to raise on her own.

Heath was also disappointed. He did not like that he had to give up his freedom without it being his choice. He began turning his back on all his ambitious dreams and became a pauper and a drunk. However, he was able to hold on to a management position for the duration of his life. Careen's hedonistic spirit was influential and dominant. Without God you can do nothing.

CHAPTER 2

The Undertows of Tradition

As Careen grew into a young woman, she tried to get her mom to understand that her hopes and dreams were different from the expectations of others—her parents, siblings, friends, and communities. But her mom could not see beyond her contented life as a wife and mother who, like her mother before her, had built a home with her husband on their own land. The hope of Careen's mother was simple: to become a grandma and to see Careen with a husband and embracing the same domestic contentment by making her home and future on Jamaican soil. Careen's mother couldn't understand Careen's yearning or her inner calling to venture beyond the familiar fulfillment as a wife and mother.

Careen's mom discouraged her dreams, just as her dad also discouraged her from venturing off the farm into things unknown. But Careen could not be happy constrained at home, nor did she know what was driving her to be so restless. She had an innovative mind that pulled her toward the larger world and possibilities of a professional career beyond familiarity. She was determined to seek a viable path to accomplish her goals and began to drive her thoughts harder toward her vision without the help or support of her parents. She bump into Beverly in town one evening and Beverly mention that she had gotten a visa, and careen should keep her ears open for the announcement, then wey you a put the boy, careen asked, me a carry him to who give him to me and lef him they. Her siblings saw Careen's future the way they saw their own: marriage, family, and the achievements of living off their land and by the carpentry and masonry of the men folks.

As though caught in a river's undertow, Careen was pulled into the dominant current of her society that led young women to become homemakers, many as unwed mothers. Careen began having babies by different fathers. It seemed to her that each time she took a promising step toward her dreams, something would happen to push her back. Still she was determined in heart and mind to keep pushing forward to answer the call of her heart that would free her from the undertow of tradition.

Careen learned that the government was giving foreign visas to those who had an sponsor under whom they would work. Careen believed this was her opportunity, her first step toward the future she had envisioned her entire life. She quickly placed herself on the path to secure a position as a nanny and a housekeeper for a family in the United States. Although the work was domestic and not the career she would eventually pursue, the migration and work opportunity was a stepping-stone that would open further opportunities for education and advancement toward a professional career.

The difficult but temporary sacrifice required was placing her five children with different family members until she could bring them to America. Her twins went to live with their dad and his family members, and the oldest and the youngest daughters stayed with her sister, who had no children of her own.

But her daughter Charlotte's father, Heath, would not allow her to be placed anywhere but in a boarding school. Fortunately Charlotte's dad knew of such a place where a woman boarded children whose parents were in different foreign countries. She would house them until they had received their visas. Charlotte spent the first year in this place, but the first year of applying for a visa is only the first step; you have to wait a second year and then reapply, paying the fees all over again, before you are approved to board the Jamaican jumbo jet as a permanent resident to your destination.

Careen did not marry any of the fathers to her children, but the men were part of the children's lives in varying degrees. Heath, Charlotte's dad, had been especially centered on Charlotte and her future since the day of the baby's birth. While he was unable to care for Charlotte himself at his home, he was unwavering in his love for her and insisted on what he believed was best for her at any given time or point of contention with Careen. So Charlotte was placed in the boarding school for what was supposed to be one year until her departure for America. Because of the undertow of tradition, Charlotte spent another year in Jamaica in the visa procurement process, and there were no extra funds to keep her in the boarding school.

She went to live with her aunt. Heath had spoken with her about Charlotte coming to live with her and her two other sisters. Her aunt quickly made space, knowing that this process was not lengthy and all funds must be on hand. Besides, this arrangement allowed her to bond with her youngest sister. She was able to teach her to read and write. She was writing her ABCs before she left Jamaica. Without access to paper and not having gotten a slate as yet, she taught her by using the clay earth.

The clay earth was hard and accustomed to be written on it held the alphabeth or what ever you write charlotte protested when it was time to leave her little sister. she clung to her aunt, not understanding the transaction that was taking place. she was a toddler when her aunt began caring for her, so she knew her aunt as Mom and call her so. her two siblings were not there, whom she had not bonded with, but God is gracious, and the bonding that was created by God was not an accident. Charlotte did not understand Gods' plan as to why it wasn't all three of us going on this plane, but her dad tried explaining and calmed her to the point of getting her in the car. her aunt waved from the gate of the house, knowing she would not see her for a very long time.

Trace Charlottes' cousin that was staying at the house her mom had gotten her visa and she had just left Jamaica to be with her mom said," Aunty is family oriented and believed in making space for family".

She lived in a one-bedroom apartment, and during our stay, she tried to instill values that would keep us alive, whether in our professional or personal lives. She taught her sister Karen to cook. Her sister loved her new skill until she put the meat in the pot of hot oil without first blotting the excess water from the meat. It sprinkled tiny oil droplets from the pot that frightened Karen, and she had to walk around looking as though she had brown freckles on her light skin face. This experience was informative to her (and to me also) that hot oil does not like water. Karen was upset for months that the oil should have not splashed on her, No one would be able to see the freckles on you she said; besides, they only lasted a few months.

Charlotte had a distant aunt that she had spent time with while her mom was in Jamaica. This was who Careen wanted her to live with while she went to America, but her dad would not hear of it. When she was attending the 5th and 6th grade, she had lived with this aunt in her large house, one section of which was government property and functioned as the district post office. Careen had asked her aunt why the large gate was in a section of the living room her aunt had told her. When Aunty opened the post office, an iron gate separated the home from the post office, and no one was allowed beyond the gate, her aunt opened the gate at a certain time and closed it at a certain time. She also had a caretaker for the home who came at breakfast time and stayed through lunch and supper. He came every morning; you never saw him when he came, but you always saw him when he went down the hill and around the corner. He prepared the three meals and snack, and wash and keep the house clean.

After closing the post office, by 4pm as the evening gets dark aunty allowed us to sit with her on the front porch as she wait for the neighbors who would have not gotten their mail the country bus arrived around seven pm sometimes eight pm, the other little girl whose name was charlotte aunty had gotten her from a lady who had too many children. Aunty would sit on the porch to see and talk with the passing neighbors as they got off the country bus from town heading to their own homes. She would hand mail to recipients and hold conversation with those getting off the country bus coming in from the market or coming into the gate to talk or get their mail.

During these lengthy visits, it got darker, and in the country in the 1960s there were no street lights. First the mosquitoes would sting you, and if you stayed outside, these flies with light around their heads, the peenie wallies, would gather and give so much light you didn't need streetlights. Some nights they shone so bright you could see who was gathered together from a distance These peenie wallies gathered together to give light when people stood or sat around in the dark. You always knew how many crowds were gathered outside; you could see the circles of lights. The mosquitoes would annoy you at first, but then when the light came, the mosquitoes would only sting you once in a while.

One day charlotte decided to tour the house after living there a month. It was huge, with two living rooms and several doors leading to the outside. Even her bedroom had one. Four bedrooms each had a door leading to the outside. She was fascinated by the many entrances the house had. her bedroom was on the east side of the house; the sun would rise and always shine right on her bed. On school days she was always up, dressed, and ready, listening for the voices of the children as they gathered at the entrance to begin the mile walk through the forest to the only school.

On other days she would rise, wash her face, and get a knife and lie in the fullest orange tree. She would get a handful of bird apples and lay in the trees, bird apples are shape like pears they have red thin skin and are sweet they are not meaty they have a bite just like the pears switching from apples to oranges most of the morning, lying in wait to see the help for the lady next door as she maneuvered her duties. After a while the help would arrive. she could see her work outside but could only imagine it inside.

One day she had washed a large white bedspread with a printed design on it, and she had hung it on the line. The lady of the house came outside and inspected the spread. She yanked it off the line and smeared it in the dirt. Then she told the girl to get it white. The girl was crying and picked up the spread and began washing it. After the lady went inside, charlotte asked the girl why was she rewashing such a big spread after the lady smeared it in the dirt. The girl said she needed the money. From that day charlotte only watched and never spoke to the girl again.

she saw her get gasoline from the tank. She put the hose in her mouth and pulled until her mouth was full of gasoline. Then she aimed the hose in a container to fill it with gasoline. This was a summer home for the neighbor, and her vacation time was over. The lady went back to where she'd come from, and that was the end of the help. charlotte never saw the girl again.

While she lived with her aunt in Kingston, she wanted to give us each stability in our lives. She asked charlotte one day to clean her bedroom. As she had never worked but only watched other people as they worked, I'd never seen anyone clean a room or the inside of a house. She dusted, made the bed, and swept and shined the floor. After we had eaten supper, her aunt said, "Charlotte, I am going to check the room you cleaned." She put on a white glove and began moving the furniture away from the wall she ran her finger along the base board and showed her finger to charlotte; it was dirty. She said, "This room is not clean." Aunty went outside and got some dirt and sprinkled it on the floor. Then she said, "Go and clean the room."

Charlotte told her no, she was not cleaning it up. She decided she was not sleeping in the house unless charlotte cleaned the room. She put her suitcase of clothes outside. charlotte picked it up and headed out the gate. she went to her father's house, but he did not want her to even spend the night there because of contentions he did not want her involved in. He gave her some money, and she went out the door and through his gate. she went to her youngest sister father's house, because it was getting dark. He was not at home, but his wife was, she told her to stay for the night. While it was still night, he came to charlotte room. We had a talk, and charlotte decided it was best not to spend another night.

When the sun rose in the morning, charlotte was already gone. She had caught the country bus in search of her aunt, but she had been transferred to another post office in another part of the country. charlotte did not seek her any further, because a lady she talked to in the nearby district told her to stay with her and not to go looking through the countryside for her aunt. she stayed at the stranger lady's house. She and her daughter went to town daily to work. After she'd stayed at their house a couple of months, they started whispering and acting weird. They came home one day and asked charlotte to go in the house and not come out until they call her. This woman had appeared in the yard. They sat her down with her back toward the house.

she had given up on going to America and never spoke of it. she had even put her aunt and her sisters out of her thoughts. As a result, she did not recognize her aunt from the back. her aunt her dad and sister, however, had been looking for her. They put charlotte picture in the *Jamaica Star*, the evening newspaper that everybody reads. The lady and her daughter had read the *Star* and hid the paper from her sight. They contacted her aunt to let her know she was okay and was living with them. her aunt came right over.

When they called her outside, they had spread out in case she started running. They were ready to catch her, but it had been so long, and her stay at this stranger's house was so unique and pleasant. Besides, living in the country was where her heart was, among the trees and the rivers. The lady had called her son one day and warned him that he should not have anything to do with her and that she was to stay in the house until further notice That was startling information for her as she listened to it. she was a stranger to this family, yet she put charlotte under the protection her dad would have required from her mom against any male company.

Then her aunt showed up saying her visa had been approved a couple of days ago, and she needed to come with her. The lady walked up to her and asked her to go to her mother. She said the process had been long, but now the embassy had given the approval, and it was time to leave Jamaica. she thanked and said goodbye to two really good people. From the moment she asked her to stay instead of looking for her aunt, she felt the hands of protection around her. It was an enclosing or encasing presence.

When she got to Kingston, her aunt was glad to be able to put both her and her sister Karen on the plane. She just kept rehearsing the process of posting the picture in the *Star*; charlotte only sat and listened. she did not know how to thank God, but He knew how to protect her. Charlotte baby sister and her aunt did not travel with them to the airport; there was just enough space in the little car for her, her sister, her dad, and the driver, her dad's friend.

CHAPTER 3

Joan a.k.a. Charlotte

As a child her pet name was Joan. her mother wanted to name her after her own mother, Joanie. At the time of her birth, her dad did not look favorable on her grandmother Joanie. He declared that was not the name of his newborn, and the baby would be named Charlotte. her mom and aunts insisted that she should be named Joan, in honor of their mom, but Dad had an inner connection with the Lord and was following orders as to the divine direction of the life of Charlotte on the earth.

her dad never relented, he wouldn't hear of naming his daughter Joan. On her birth certificate is the legal name she will be called.

Still, her mother, and her family, and everyone who came to know charlotte as a child in Jamaica called her Joan—except for Dad. On the many occasions he visited her, he called her Charlotte.

At the age of twelve she was at last able to join her mother in the U.S. Her mother enrolled her in school under the name Charlotte. she told her teachers and classmates, "her name is Joan," but one teacher asked who Joan was and why they called her Joan. She told her teacher the story of her grandmother and her father's wish for her to be called Charlotte.

Then the teacher said, "That is what we are going to call you, Charlotte, because that is what is on your birth certificate, and we have to call you by the name you are registered under, which corresponds with your birth certificate."

she struggled with being called Charlotte. she knew the name was her birth name, the name her Dad called her, but she knew herself only as Joan and felt no ties to the name Charlotte. It was as though Charlotte was a person apart from her, a mental twin that she really didn't know and could not relate to. She knew herself as Joan, so it was hard for her at school to get used of being called Charlotte.

The transformation from Joan to Charlotte was challenging for her charlotte friends saw that she was struggling with her legal name, and they wanted to help, so at times they would call out to her, "Charlotte!" for no apparent reason. One-day she asked them, "Why are you always calling out my name for no reason?" They said they were helping her get used to her real name. Some of them were Jamaicans also and saw and knew the struggle to transform from a pet name.

Over time, she began to realize that her legal name was important. she realized this name had an identity of its own, and she had to fit into this person. She balanced the new person for a while; then she began meeting people called Charlotte and realized they had that personality of who this Charlotte person was. Slowly she accepted being this person because no one would call her Joan.

she had no trees to climb. she was a tree climber, having lived in a yard in Jamaica where three trees stood by each other. They were my escape from the earth. she climbed in those trees and walked from one tree to the next without getting down from the trees. She felt relaxed to be in the trees. It made her feel close to heaven, although she did not understand the connection or the desire or yearning. Her spiritual past, her memory of a preexisting life, had not come into focus as a child.

There was no one to play marbles with. she had a neighbor whose mom would buy him the prettiest designs of marbles. The colors swirled in them. He always brought them outside to play. She would draw a circle, and he would place them in the circle. We took turns knocking them from the circle, and when we were called in for our supper, charlotte had collected most of his marbles. His mom always knocked on the door to get the marbles back, and we would play again after supper.

She was athletic but did not challenge any of her strengths in the athletic field. Mom was busy, and charlotte had no other to confide in about her abilities. she loved playing baseball recreationally, but she never thought about playing professionally. She never heard of a female baseball player while living in Jamaica, and being of a competitive nature, found it difficult to play the game of basketball. One had to pass the ball to other players and become disappointed when they missed the basket. she always thought that she would have made the basket. One day when her coach explained that she had to relinquish the ball, she knew basketball was only a game for her to watch.

Over time, she began to realize that her legal name was important to her. It was at that mental milestone that she began living fully as Charlotte, leaving behind the trails of shadows that would impede her, living as though there were two of them: Joan,-a tomboy who played marbles, climbed trees, kicked stones, fought like a boy, and was extremely competitive; and Charlotte, a girl who was conservative and conscious about her surroundings and her reputation and loved fashion and a modern lifestyle. Charlotte was competitive as well, but not as much as Joan.

Like her mother, who dreamed and reached determinedly beyond her upbringing, she was a child who saw and understood things beyond the awareness of the average child her age. she possessed a spiritual gift that she didn't understand. she was told by her mom and aunts that when she was born, she arrived into the world with a white caul over her face. Babies born with such a covering are considered spiritually blessed. her dad, who had not been at the hospital when she was born, hurried to Careen's home to meet his daughter as soon as he had gotten word that she'd been born. He arrived to find Careen's family gathered outside, which is customary when there's a birth. Careen brought the newborn outside, under the trees where the family stood in the cool shade flecked by sunlight through the leaves.

When Heath first laid eyes on his daughter, he took her from Careen's arms and held his baby for a long while, looking down into her tiny face. At first he didn't speak. Neither Careen nor her family knew his intentions, but they graciously gave Heath space and time with his daughter. Only he and God knew the conversation they were having in those life-altering moments.

After a time, he raised the baby girl towards the heavens and audibly asked God to protect and guide his daughter's life. He had recognized in his silent moments of bonding that he would not be able to guide her as she should be guided, but he had strong belief in God and that God had ordained a specific path for his daughter's life. His prayer was followed by a chorus of: Amen" and everyone relaxed, pleased with his blessing over his daughter's life.

Through the years as she grew up, she had a cousin she admired. She would go to work and leave her son in their house with many books to read. He occasionally would look out the window. She was always sitting where when he looked, she was able to see his face. When his mom got home from work, she could hear her asking him what book he'd read and what he understood from reading the books. After several years of not seeing her cousin—the distance between countries was a boundary—when she saw her cousin, her thoughts were momentarily drawn back into her childhood.

When she thought about the career he chose, although she never saw the covers of his books, he had a toy that would spin, and she would look at it for a long while, though she never played with it. This cousin had great enterprise ideas about small objects that allow things to turn or spin. He orchestrated his ideas to produce many small objects of different sizes and shapes that connected to other objects. Today he is involved with one of Jamaica's top leading pipe networking organizations.

charlotte mom would take her and her sister to visit another cousin when she came home to visit. She was in college to be a nurse. she never saw her books either, but she wore a white uniform, white shoes, and a white cap. After some time, she was told her cousin had left Jamaica for England.

These are some of the memories she keep in her head. Then when that lady with the long blond hair came across the yard and told her that in her latter years, God would bless her, she did not understand what any of that meant. But she always felt content, even as she reflect she should not have been content, but she was and still am.

One day her sister Karen's sickle cell had attacked her, and she was in pain. Mom had stayed home from work, but the next day she told her charlotte would stay home from school because she had said she could not stay home another day from work, and Karen would be left alone. Because she was worried, charlotte agreed to volunteered to stay. Karen slept most of the morning, and by noon she had begun stirring. Charlotte went to Mom's room where Karen spent her nights and days. She had woken from her sleep; the medication the doctor had prescribed for her had completed its effect, and she was feeling better. she sat on Mom's bed, and Karen put her head in charlotte lap. She turned her head slightly, looking up, and said to her, "I can't stand black people."

charlotte was stunned by Karen's remark and was at a loss for words. As she looked down at her pale face, weary from the sickle attacks and the injustices of life that she carried, she was not sure how to respond.

Karen and her often had soul-to-soul conversations, but her adamant statement didn't sound to her like an invitation to talk but rather an accusation. Cautiously she responded with a hint of defensiveness: "am I not black. I could be in school right now, but I stayed home with you, and this is the thanks to get?"

Karen quickly explained, "I don't mean you or Mom ... but I can't stand black people," she confessed. She didn't explain to her why she couldn't stand black people, and she didn't push her. she saw her statement as veiled, as though she needed to tell her some secret but felt that she could not explain herself without some fear of betrayal of trust and getting into trouble with her mother.

Karen always had bitter, angry feelings—resentment over what should have been a treat and a delight for both of us, to have our dads visit us. She felt different within herself and was not able to bring herself up from the darkness. She did not want to be classified as white. If the lighter skin had it so well, then where was her dad to complete her growing status? She struggled with that identity. And Cleve to be angry and bitter inside, Karen grew with the stigma "You're black, I'm white," a stigma our mom tried to counter with the assurance that life would be better and easier for Karen because of her light complexion. Further, she also told Karen that the darker skin people had a harder time trying to be independent and getting a good job.

That statement really upset Karen. She believed our mother was trying to tear charlotte down, the only person she felt was her true confidant in life, the one person Karen shared most of her deepest thoughts with.

Uncertain how to respond, she just looked down at Karen, feeling a mix of compassion and emotion, thinking that now, being in America, Karen would be able to see other people her color in her situation and not be bombarded with the dominant African color. She might now get in touch with her inner person and feel connected with some part of who she needed to develop as a person. Each time her dad came to visit, she said to him, "Put Karen in your lap so she can sit on your lap."

Those feelings of loss and yearning for Karen resurfaced as she looked down at her. And again she considered the fact that Karen had no father figure, no relationship with the man who fathered her, and a mother who was struggling with the discomfort of her child feeling as she grew and developed, asking, "How can I separate my personalities when I don't know my design, who I am, or what I should do?" These are some of the questions Karen would put to charlotte after her dad left for the evening: "You can make choices, you can choose to be in church, you can choose to be a drunk, you can become an idol, but who am I, and what choices can I make?"

In answer to these conscious thoughts and questions, Mom would say to her the most obvious: "Don't worry so much about how life will be for you. Your skin is light, and you will have a better chance in life than the darker skin." This was no consolation to Karen who loved her sister. She only viewed the statements as a wedge to separate what reality she knew all her life.

One day in Kingston, when Karen and charlotte were staying with their aunt, they were in the backyard. charlotte was playing in the mud making mud pies while Karen was washing and hanging clothes on the line. Then, from the corner of her eye, she saw movement. she stopped and looked up toward the movements to see a white woman with long, flowing blond hair coming out from the door of a neighbor and walking across the yard. she knew the neighbor was not at home; this was a workday, but this white woman came out of her door, walked across the yard, and sat on the edge of the stone basin. charlotte walked over to her and leaned against her leg. Karen was slow in coming; she knew this woman came from a door where no one was home, and the door was not ajar at any given time. She drew close and stopped about a foot away.

The woman began talking. First she told Karen all the things she would do that were not pleasing to the Lord, saying that the Lord would be angry about the things she chose to do, especially to charlotte. Neither Karen nor charlotte questioned her.

Then she turned to charlotte and said, "The Lord will bless you in your latter days. He will see all you have done, and He will reward you." Then she said, "You will anger the Lord somewhat in things you choose to do, but it is for a short time."

All the while this woman was talking she was worried for her safety in the backyard of a tenement house in Kingston 10. charlotte was petrified some of the boys might see the woman, but you could not see from the front gate directly to the backyard. she was relieved when she got through talking and left the way she had come. We were distracted talking to each other when she made her final disappearance, and when we turned to look, she was gone. charlotte tried to memorize what the woman had said, but she was so petrified for her safety that the only thing that stuck with her was that she would anger the Lord. she purposed within herself that she would refrain from this thing that would cause God to be angry.

After she had come to the United States and ventured into things unknown, she quickly remembered the separation of people and the disapproval of her dad when her mom would tell him whom we had visited in her family for the weekend. At first she did not understand why she could not visit or stay for any length of time with family members, until after coming to the States she curiously looked into the other world and felt its air of disapproval. Then she remembered the words of the woman who came to the backyard, saying she would displease God but for a short while, and she remembered the voice of God when she came off the plane and had gotten to mountclair new jersey she was laying in her room and had fallen asleep she opened her eyes and lift her head to look out the window there was this white powder every where there was a little tree and the powder layed on the limbs heavily the branches bowed to the ground I layed my head on the bed thinking about the dog cradeled in his dog house, then a voice began speaking to me I gave it my complete attention, and He spoke to charlotte as she lay on her bed in her room, saying, "Now your dad is not with you, you have to be mindful where you go, what you do, and places you visit." God had told her, "Do not entertain the spirits of mediums or palm readers. Don't be burning candles in incense for luck or protection." she had done these things until she remembered the words of prophecy because it was an experience she had not had before learning that it was an evil action in the sight of God. This had come to her from the woman and God Himself; it was this revelation that made her cross over and walk the side of the road where the air was fresh and clear. This experience opened her eyes as what is accepted and what causes God to frown

CHAPTER 4

A New Way of Life

As Karen entered high school and charlotte started junior high, Careen told us she did not want us to bring any boys to the house. But Karen had seen a boy that she was interested in and wanted to invite him to the house. She told me she wanted to invite this boy to the house to help her with her homework. she said, "Why don't you stop over his house?" She said she was not comfortable with that idea. "Okay," she said, "there could be a potential problem if no one is at his house." I reminded her about Mom's rule. Karen said she would take care of it; she did not question her. Concerned, charlotte conceded, "Just make sure he's gone before Mom gets home."

Karen agreed.

When the time came for the boy to leave, Karen had decided that he should stay longer; she was not finished with the project she was working on. Charlotte reminded her again, but Karen kept talking with the boy until Mom walked up the stairs. She asked the boy to leave, which Karen could have done minutes before, but Karen had a tumultuous burden she was carrying and wanted to finish the conversation with the boy, expressing her feelings. Karen had faced her biggest demon, to challenge Careen's orders, but how was charlotte to view this?

For every action there is a reaction. Careen was very angry. Although Karen was the one who had disobeyed, Careen took her anger out on charlotte. She came at her wielding a spike-heel shoe like a sword. charlotte was trying to get away from the physical threat and fell near the top of the

26

stairs holding on to the post of the stairs down, down, to the next floor. In Careen's anger she kicked charlotte, and she tumbled down the long flight of steps. As soon as she hit the bottom step, her hand was mysteriously placed on the doorknob. she struggled to her feet, twisted the knob, and stepped out the door into the hall that led to the street. And she kept on walking, right out of her family's life and onto the path designed for her growth, the journey to reunite her with Christ.

she walked until it was nearly dark outside. she knew she could not find her way around Montclair, New Jersey, being a fairly new resident in the area, so she went to a neighbor, an older woman who had no children, just herself and her husband. When she saw how bruised she was, she took her inside and told her she could stay for the night, but they were not able to take care of her for an extended time she thanked them, and along with a good night's sleep she had time to think.

she woke the next morning with a fresh idea. she ate the breakfast waiting for her, thanked the elderly couple again, and left for Newark, where CiCi was living. This was a friend of her mother who had told Karen and her that if they needed her at any time, we could come to her. When CiCi opened the door, she saw charlotte and her bruises. She welcomed her into her home to stay as long as she needed. CiCi was not a churchgoer, but the Lord allowed her to stay long enough to view a life pattern that He rejected but knew she would be able to endure.

It was her dad also who had instilled in her the strength to make tough decisions in life and to stand on her own two feet when he would come over to visit he would stay in the yard under the big tree with the most leaves she was not allowed to hug him, if she stayed near him she had to stand. Living in Newark and being on her own was all new to her. There were so many things to become familiar with. Like the veil that had covered Moses' face,-separating him in spirit from the Israelites-when he had come down from the mountain bearing the tablets of God's commandments, she felt veiled from her family. She was entering a new path where God alone was her protection and her provider.

When you accept Jesus as your Savior, God places His spirit in you to guide you. No matter what circumstances you encounter, He is there with you. He sets you apart from the things and people of this world and cares for you as His beloved child. Even when you're physically alone or feel alone, you can trust your heavenly Father is with you and that He is faithful to His promise to carry you from your bondage—a bondage Karen knew very well.

Jesus did not want charlotte to continue living in the enemy camp. He designed an escape and propelled her toward the Promised Land He had designed for her path and her life; the life she had just left was a temporary stay. God had made these arrangements to bring her to the United States to complete His mission in her and for her. He will propel you to simply stay on the path of His leading and follow Him on that divine path instead of the path of this world, He will lead you into His divine will and purpose for your life. He is the one true protector and provider of your life, the one you can fully trust to never leave you or forsake you. No matter how you have suffered or sinned, He heals and forgives those who call on the name of His Son, Jesus, in faith.

Jesus, speaking to the disciples of His imminent ascension into heaven, said, "It is for your good that I am going away. Unless I go away, the Advocate [God's Spirit] will not come to you; but if I go, I will send him to you …. I have much to say to you, more than you can now bear. But when he, the spirit of truth, comes, he will guide you into all the truth" (John 16:7, 12–13).

CiCi registered charlotte in the nearby junior high school. she attended school daily when it was open and loved going to school. she received good grades, which helped boost her morale to get up in the morning and be in her seat by the time the school bell rang. CiCi saw that charlotte did not have adequate clothing for a young girl attending school, so she took her shopping. When she got home and was trying on her clothes, she noticed that on one of her favorite TV shows, the girl had on one of her outfits. This really made her feel good, to know she was choosing the right fashion.

One evening charlotte came home from school, and Karen was there at CiCi's house. This was a surprise to her. When she asked what happened, she said she could not stay in Montclair living away from her, so the decision was made for her to move in and live with CiCi. During this time of separation our mother had transferred to Connecticut; another arrangement of God.

Meanwhile, CiCi had been trying to get some help with funds to buy more clothes and food. This called for a hearing by the judge. When charlott went to the judge, he invited her into his chambers. she explained that she did not want to live with her mom. The judge said if she continued her good grades, she could stay with CiCi, but along the way the judge arranged for her to attend school in Germantown, at the Catholic girls' school. While the decision was in process, she kept on attending school every day and loved it. her grades were good, and there were many young people her age and older. Although she loved her school and the diversity of students that attended, she only befriended a couple of the students; most of them were Puerto Ricans and spoke their native Spanish. she was a people watcher and liked to see what made people react and how they react to their stimuli.

Newark was very different from Montclair. There she had hear nothing about Martin Luther King or "black power," as she was now exposed to. she lived two blocks from the school. Walking home from school, she would arrive before the school bus passed on CiCi's busy street. From inside her home, charlotte would look out the window as the bus passed and see kids' fists raised outside the bus windows and hear them yelling, "I am black and I am proud!"

One day after school she asked a couple of kids why they said those words and raised their fists. Their answer was simply that others were doing it, so they did. That vague answer was not enough information for her to give their repeated behavior a second thought. However, the Voice within her restrained her and advised her not to become a part of their movement, He let it be known to her, that people were lacking knowledge and that she should not follow their pattern.

> Do not conform to the pattern of this world but be
> transformed by the renewing of your mind. Then you will
> be able to test and approve what God's will is – his good,
> pleasing and perfect will. (Romans 12:2)

One day CiCi received a letter from the judge. The girls' school in Germantown had an opening, and her name was next on the list. A social worker showed up and loaded charlotte into the car, and off we went to Germantown. she had left Karen behind again, but she had met an Indian boy, and he was good to her. So she had company while she stayed at CiCi's house.

she heard many different songs as we traveled on the road. The social worker had her radio tuned to the popular station for the East Coast. The American songs came over the radio, separating her from her heritage and placing her in a new time frame and a new way of life and living. As we traveled toward Germantown, by the time we got there, she could practically sing most of the songs: "Ooh Child, Things Are Gonna Get Easier," "ABC," and "That Girl."

After getting to Germantown, we pulled up to this huge gate. The social worker said she would not have to worry; everything was provided here for her. The school was downstairs; the cafeteria was buffet style for every meal. The dentist visited on certain days and came right into the building. The church where mass was held was also in the building, but these priests were different from the ones she knew. When Communion came, you sipped from this large cup. The wine was so strong, she staggered from the church; that was the first and last time she had Communion while she stayed in Germantown.

When we had break time, we smoked cigarettes. That became a habit, but after she left Germantown, God had a plan to get her focus closer to His revelation. He took away the habit as if she had been holding something for another person; it was gone instantly. God was conditioning Charlotte, for closer walk with him.

One day a friend came so we could ride around for the evening on the back roads of New Canaan, Connecticut. As we traveled the need for a cigarette was pressing. she took a cigarette and lit it. Then a voice said, "Throw that away." she looked over at the driver, who looked more concerned about his driving than her lighting a cigarette. She took a puff of the cigarette, and her vision went black; she couldn't see anything. she struggled to shake the darkness from her eyes.

Then she said, "If you did not want me to smoke in the car, you should have said so," but the driver looked confused at her statement. He was raised in a Christian home and knew more than she, about God and His deliverance. He perceived God was dealing with her to give up the cigarettes, and as she continued on the subject, he assumed God was doing a work in her. He began asking her to throw away her cigarettes. she mentioned how many cigarettes she had, and he said to throw them all away. she began with the pack in her hand; then she got the pack from her pocket and the one from her pocketbook. she did it slowly, but soon she had thrown them all out the window as the car moved down the road, and after that evening she had no desire for a cigarette. God had delivered her completely.

At the school we did not have rooms. We slept on beds in an open dormitory. You could stand anywhere in the vast room and see everyone at once. she stayed there for two winters. But she put on weight, which was not good; she had to lose the weight.

Her mom had petitioned the court that she had moved to another state and had a lovely place all ready for her daughter to come home to. Upon hearing this, she believed her sister and her would be sharing a room on our own beds.

The courts told Mom they did not have a hold on charlotte. she had been placed there because there was enough space and they wanted to keep her safe. And she could take charlotte as soon as she could provide a way to transport her there. Soon Mom showed up, and they left Germantown heading for Connecticut.

Karen was already there and had made friends. Mom and charlotte headed into the condominium, and she stood still. The condo was unique and designed for Mom. After observing the space, she began to reflect on her mom and remembered she only provide enough space for herself; if you needed to reside at her place, you had to humble yourself of all your feelings. she did not have the desire to return to Germantown. However moving back to Germantown would impede the Lords' work. A social worker showed up and told her about this home that housed young teenagers. She asked if she wanted to try living there. Although Mom's condo was in a quiet suburban cul-de-sac and tucked away from the activity of the neighborhood, she accepted the offer to live elsewhere.

she lived there one year and learned to eat eggplant with cheese. That big purple vegetable she now cook for herself; if she had not lived with that family, she would walk right past the plant in the grocery store. she enjoyed her stay at the home. she walked away with new ideas and fresh thoughts—and still all this living without anyone ever mentioning anything about Jesus or going to church. Charlotte began remembering the voice He speaks of not conforming to the pattern of this world, but if you do not train up a child to reverence God and love Him, you have no other hope but to conform to a pattern of survival, which is food, clothing, and a place to live, and all this through the process of education and economic patterns.

she had thoughts of one day attending medical school and working as an oncologist or in lab doing research. she envisioned herself in the lab when a cure for the AIDS virus was discovered she was apart of the group. she also thought about human medical intervention in relationship to one's faith in God. she considered how some cures for the body might drive mankind further from dependency on the Lord, Jesus Christ.

These thoughts led her to remember that this world is not home to those who believe in Jesus. she remembered from the passage of John 14:1–4 that Jesus had ascended up into heaven after His resurrection from death, to prepare a place in heaven for His followers and that we must believe that He will return for us. Charlotte remember the word mingle, the Lord had spoken to her to go and mingle at first she did not know what to think of the word, then she said this experience she has had from the time she flew down the stairs, living at cici house going to Germantown, now coming to Connecticut has got to be how you mingle.

she did well in school throughout the junior high years. she was a straight-A-student. But the adjustment to high school weighed heavily on her mind and impacted her ability to succeed academically as she had in the past. she felt lost traveling through hallways and changing classes, and she felt lost in the adjustment she had to make she did not fit in, nothing seem appropriate what she thrive for was against the path that was design, she was heading in the path of rhetoric philosophy with no attachment to the cross. What would she have known, what would she have testified to. When the mind is close there is no testifying she did not like the rushing and dashing through the halls between classes to get to her locker and then to the next class. she'd forget a book, leaving it in her locker, and a teacher would think her irresponsible. This weighed heavy on her mind.

Typically, she would have been attentive to the lessons, but she was distracted by trying to compose herself after each mishap. she was caught in a downward spiral. Unlike Junior high, she also found herself fishing through the personality of each teacher in an effort to understand the lessons. she didn't want to mingle with other students, to become part of such a crowded environment, because she had difficulty processing the methodology of high school. It contained such a diverse group of young people and multiple teachers that the situation overwhelmed her. Instead of excelling as she was accustomed to doing, she felt safer sitting quietly somewhere and wait for her mind to catch up to the changes and swirl of activity around her. Her peers and teachers wanted her to immediately acclimate and be up to speed with their expectations, but she was unable.

For literature studies, the class was reading *White Fang* by Jack London. she tried to read along and process the contents, but all she seemed able to do was simply hold the book as if her mind had become frozen. Consequently, she'd walk the hallways feeling guilty that she was not completing the book assignment. In the end, she did not graduate high school. Charlotte thought about her brother was vague, she knew she felt different but she could not connect to what the separation was and what it was that made her feel unconnected to her peers and the things they do for enjoyment, living this life was difficult or almost impossible for Charlotte she could not connect and was not connecting.

The friend Karen made was also Jamaican. Most of the people in the community and surrounding areas were Jamaicans. her sister's friend lived a few blocks from Mom's condo, also in a conservative neighborhood in a single family rental home where she occupied the basement apartment of her moms' home. As we were high school seniors, we did not have jobs or own cars in the early 1970s; we walked the sidewalk.

There were people of all nationalities, a hand full of elderly some graduates from college the teenagers and preteens, like the graduates from last year and the year before. Some walk with baby strollers or their pets. It was a family-friendly atmosphere, not only with the junior highs but also with the high school students and new immigrants. Our transportation was strolling or else taking the bus or a taxi. Mostly we strolled. Days and evenings in Connecticut were peaceful; the atmosphere was pleasant for anyone to be out of their house and on the sidewalk the sea breeze always blow a welcoming cool air with the aroma of ocean air. You'd meet new people along with residents who had lived in Connecticut much longer than the longest resident could remember. By strolling you saw new and improved stores and new businesses being introduced. You were a part of the shopping experience and the changes. We loved strolling through the streets, when we drive we only see the new developments we are not interactive and knowing the owners getting to greet and know our business owners sitting in the shops for café or a donut is a wonderful feeling.

Her sister's best friend's mom was acquainted with karen mom; who also knew the sister of the mom she was also an acquaintance, of the mom and she had several sons. Desmond, another of her sons, was granted his American visa and arrived into the United States. Word quickly got from home to home that another person had gotten approval to be in the United States. Because of all these acquaintances, the single females made themselves available, and you could hear the buzz around town about who would be the first to have a date with the new arrival.

charlotte stood back looking at the commotion but found that she was in the very center of the decision. *The Godfather* was the most popular movie playing, and everybody had made plans to see the movie. Paula, Karen's best friend, called her to ask if she wanted to go to the movies. Then she said, "You just came into town; come and go with us." An odd number of people had been invited, so after we got inside the theater, charlotte placed herself where Paula would be seated next to the new arrival, Desmond. But he waited until everyone was seated; then, being quite tall in stature, he stepped over the seat between Paula and charlotte and stood waited until the movie started then told Paula to move over there was no place for charlotte to move the theatre was pack he sat between us.

This was awkward. she was a third wheel, but when he moved Paula and took her seat instead, charlotte felt out of place. he had brothers, but this was a different setting. We were at the movies, and he chose to sit next to charlotte. Although she sat quietly, he always turned his head toward her when he spoke, so she reminded him that Paula was on his other side, and he asked what that meant, she said, "You know, she is interested in you."

But he said, "I'm interested in who I am interested in." After the movie we were exchanging names and numbers and saying things like "See you tomorrow."

she didn't know what a boyfriend was except from what she saw on television. Between Dad's watchful eyes and the Catholic girls' school, she had been sheltered, and everything was new. she was, she had no idea what to do. Desmond and her kept seeing each other as the days became weeks and then months and they became very intimate. she was still in high school, and he was looking to enter college.

First she was trying to understand White people and their worldview. When she entered school, they had an attitude that conveyed that they felt invincible and untouchable about life. They walked through the halls of school as though they knew why they existed. she was focused on her peers because the teachers were more conservative. Just as she focused on that, it started to snow, and she wanted the perception of snow: why must it snow? Everything seems to stop being what it appears to be, and another form takes control. You are cloaked in garments against shivering cold.

Before she could present this argument to the Lord, a greater interruption to her calculation found her in Germantown, in a Catholic school for girls, where everything happened within its walls. she no longer had to struggle with the snow and with white people and their thoughts of invincibility; what she was now dealing with was all encompassed within a struggle, and their attitude was very different now she had encountered another set of white people or who complexion was lighter than colored people some were from Hungary. They were needing nurturing; they wanted someone to hear about their struggle, and her ingenuity was put on hold. Compassion overwhelmed her to respond to the needs of hurting people. Although she was still a teen, she became an ear. Yet the voice of God was calmly and quietly saying, "Be not easily dismayed." The voice of the Lord says, "Learn not the way of the heathen, and be not dismayed at their sayings" (similar to Jeremiah 10:2).

she was missing her dad there was a lot to talk about there was a lot she saw. she wanted to call him; she had not heard from him and did not know how to get in touch with him. she needed to talk with him she didn't, know his phone number, but he would have wanted her to write, and she did not like writing. but changes in her life gave her hope to push on a little further without calling him. she wish she had called him; it is always these crossroads, when the light is dim, that we need to turn on the floodlight. she began to understand how God allows people a certain amount of leeway. Then He reels them back in. This simplifies a testing of our obedience, since it's making us a bride prepared to dine with her groom.

God desires us to grow and multiply, not only in our reproductive ability but in our intellect. But He does not want us driven so deep in research that it replaces praise and worship, taking away our time for Him.

God wanted her complete trust in Him. He wants each of us to rely on Him and ask Him for directions, for only He knows what we are searching for and can fully what we see only dimly. By leaning on others, we will always be like the children in the wilderness, circling Mount Sinai and unable to find a way.

At sixteen she was pregnant. Desmond and charlotte had spent too many lengthy hours together. His mom had called us into her private living room to tell us we should not be alone so often, but she was already pregnant and could not keep her eyes open for sleepiness. His older brother had a wedding reception party, and charlotte was not able to stay wake long enough to go to the party, which was in the next rooms. There were several visitors, and the family who produced the music wanted to continue the party at their house and asked Desmond to help carry the equipment. she did not want Desmond to leave the house; besides, there were more than enough men at the party to assist with the transport of the equipment.

Desmond came and said he was going to help them with the equipment. she asked him whether they was already enough help available, but he said he just wanted to go, and he would be right back. she rolled over and fell asleep. It was when he came in early in the morning that she woke up.

House parties are very common among Caribbean families, and these Jamaican house parties usually last till all hours this way, so she did not question him. He wanted to be a part of a group that she was not comfortable with. His mother was positive and encouraged him toward education, and he set out to gain a master's degree in mechanical engineering. she knew that he was seeking himself, and with his school schedule and his wanting the crowd, we drifted apart; there was no room except for his studies. He still came over and visited with me, but the atmosphere had changed between us.

After giving birth to our daughter, charlotte began receiving welfare, and they required paternity testing. Desmond and her had it done for our daughter, and he said he was sorry he had been difficult and would sign the papers for her to carry his last name. We went to the bank, had the papers notarized, and submitted them to the court, and that was how she carried his last name.

she got an apartment together with her sister Karen and the oldest daughter of a close friend of their mom. We worked and partied and took care of ourselves as best we could. she had met a guy, John, who became her boyfriend. He was just coming from Vietnam. We were together three months, and then she became pregnant again. she suggested to him that we should get married, but he told her no; he had issues and did not want to have her carry more than she already was carrying. We had a son, and we stayed together six years. Four months after we separated, he overdosed and could not be resuscitated.

During our six years John's twin brother would come to the house. One day he said to me, "Charlotte, whenever I come to the house, John always takes off to the bathroom and stays gone for a long time. Why do you never ask where he is or go looking for him?"

charlotte always thought it was break time. John and charlotte was so close that when she went to work, he walked her there. When she came home from work, sometimes he walked with her, and other times he had a bathtub full of hot soapy water ready for her to relax in. Then after supper, which he cooked, we would sit on the front porch watching the cars and latecomers going home from work. Yes, when his twin came over, it was break time; she did not worry or need to look for him. All her needs had been met.

John had made it clear that he had issues from serving with the Marines in Special Forces. He had become addicted to drugs and still had shrapnel in his head from explosive debris. Although she had longed and prayed to be married, she knew John was not the one she would make a home and life with as husband and wife legally. During her pregnancy, she heard from the Lord in response to her prayers and desire for a husband. *It is not yet the time*, she heard in her spirit. By the time our son was born, she was settled in her heart about being a single mother. Years later she looked back on that time with greater understanding. After reading the story of Ezekiel and his wife.

she believe God did not want her stagnant in a marriage He had not ordained. Therefore He did not grant her the blessing of marriage at that time. she needed to go through that season of trials to be open to learn more about Christ and what it means to live a life sold out to Him rather than to a human being, a husband. Being active in church with other believers, she experienced how valuable, important, and sweet it is to be surrounded by those who are also sold out to Christ. she was learning

God's instructions through time in His word and with other believers, and she was learning how to stand firmly rooted in Christ rather than in others. she learned by faith in trials that, no matter which way the wind blows or what trials and tests come, God is there, and He remains faithful.

Some come to God by their own desire and others through life's adversities, which discourage and tamper with faith. Then they cry out to God for help. He is seeking those who will not turn from their faith in Him.

When the winds of adversity and temptation blow, He is seeking those who will stand firm in allegiance to Him regardless of life's hardship and temptations. Although living for Christ is like the sun shining through a lattice of tree leaves—for in this life "we see only a reflection as in a mirror" (1 Corinthians 13:12)—believers must focus on eternity and keep the faith, believing that our work here on earth is to build up treasures not in this world but in heaven. We are surviving this life according to the demands of economics while waiting in faith for heavenly treasures.

> Do not store up for yourselves treasures on earth,
> where moths and vermin destroy, and where thieves break
> in and steal. But store up for yourselves treasures in heaven,
> where moths and vermin do not destroy, and where thieves
> do not break in and steal. For where your treasure is, there
> your heart will be also. (Matthew 6:19–21)

With two children to care for, she had to file for low-income housing. The application was approved, and she was able to secure a two-bedroom apartment. she was comfortable. she did not like going to Jamaican parties—or any party, for that matter. she loved Jamaican music she often play Jamaican gospel reggae, and you could oftentimes hear the rhythm coming from her apartment. For the most part, she was a loner who liked to create an aura where the Spirit of God is welcome and she could meditate on Him and His Word. Amid noise, confusion, and people with unapproachable spirits, her peaceful aura would be broken, and she would feel the need to cleanse her surroundings, to restore the peaceful aura. It was like spring cleaning: she would literally wash the walls, scrub the floors, and steam-clean the imprints from her couch. she loved the apartment she and her children had gained, and she worked hard to keep it approachable for the Lord at any time.

Her son would race through the hallways, sliding in his socks, but her daughter would get her favorite toy and sit on the sofa. she always admired how peaceful and obedient she was. As a child rosemary never presented herself as if she was afraid of her home. charlotte saw her keeping it clean, and it seemed to her she wanted to play with her toys without making a mess.

Several years later, charlotte overheard rosemary one day talking with her friend on the phone. "Well!" she said, which caught charlotte attention. "My mom kept the house so clean, I could see my face in her floor, and I did not like walking on my face, so I stayed on the couch." Charlotte was so touched to hear the words coming from her daughter's mouth.

charlotte stood still and reflected: when you have a quiet child, you should encourage them to chat sessions. All those years, and she never knew that was how her daughter felt. The neighbor would knock on the door and ask her for something but then say, "You have water on your floor. Did you just mop?" No, there was just polish on the floor. Her home must reflect her; it may have been a low income apartment, but it was the one unit she occupied, and it should say she lived there.

On the phone, her daughter began recalling how she would use the sectional as her play area. It never bothered her; she was quiet, and she did not make a mess with her toys. Also, she always included reading books in her play. She thought she was the perfect child for choosing to sit on the furniture rather than strew playthings across the floor.

Hearing her perspective was eye-opening for her. charlotte heart felt a little crunch, because she thought she knew her daughter. she simply desired to welcome the Spirit of God, and He comes often if your house is clean from clutter. This allows an open fellowship with your heavenly Father.

She began thinking about her children's future and realized there was only one practical avenue: I had to gain a high school diploma, because college programs require a high-school diploma or GED. she looked into it and learned that tests were given on Saturdays to pass the equivalent score to get a GED.

she went there one weekend and was escorted to a room and was given a Scantron sheet and a booklet with questions and answers. she began working out the answers when the instructor said begin. After the time was up, she turned in her sheet, and they asked her to wait another week to take the other half of the test.

she received a letter in the mail saying that she had passed the English and science portion; then it was time to take the other half of the test. Once again she sat down with her booklet and answer sheet and began working on the questions and the math problems. When the time was over, she handed in her sheet to the instructor. In two weeks she received another mail saying that she had surpassed the required percent score to receive her GED. That was her beginning. God was laying a pathway for her journey.

At that time several programs were being offered in the community that could lead toward a career in the mid-1970s, The CETA word processing program intrigued her, she signed up for the program and was accepted. she was taught how to use a touch typewriter; then the word processor came out, and the instructor switched over to it. We came to class after the weekend, and each desk had a word processor. The touch was light, and this helped to increase our words per minute (wpm. We aimed for 60 wpm or better; this qualified us for graduation from the program. she took a few secretarial temp jobs and realized she did not want to type for a living, although the experience was rewarding as a personal achievement.

she heard of another program that was being offered, for court reporting; she applied for that program also and was accepted. The requirement for the program was to type 45 wpm, and she was grateful for taking the CETA typing classes. Learning court reporting was like taking a Spanish course: you have to understand the language for the program, but once you master the understanding of the language, you are on your way.

But as we were about to advance into the second level of the language, the state sent an announcement that they had to close the program. We were able to keep our machines, but that was a disappointment for many of us. That was a set back, and now we had to go and find what was out there that would be equivalent to our mind-set, that would not set us aside but give us that equal opportunity for a future as participants.

Many students lined up for the nursing programs. Although this was a rewarding program, it felt like a requirement for surviving and not as challenging. There was a crowd in that line, but over here where life is just as challenging, there are no entrance exams, and crowds are discouraging.

she tried registering at the community college for the nursing program, but each attempt to study biology was too great a challenge. The sciences were not her strong suit. Strangely, in each study session, she would find herself cross-reading scriptures with her biology book. She'd set her Bible next to the biology book and alternately read them. Most of the time she fell asleep while reading and didn't retain the science information needed to be successful in biology. Although she was simply "winging it" in the course, she remained relentless in her decision to not let go of her nursing pursuit.she struggled hard through the courses that included physiology and anatomy and somehow managed to achieve good grades. The truth was that she struggled with more than academic success; she struggled with her very existence. she constantly strived to find her purpose and the best way to maneuver through life's constant twists and turns to discover that purpose.

Each afternoon after classes, she would wait at the residential health facility where Mom worked, and we would ride home together. she began doing volunteer work throughout the facility.she would assist CNAs with any chores she could. she would take a handful of the residents who were ready to be taken out to the porch before the evening sun faded. Someone had to sit out there with them, so she sat on the porch with the residents. Some of them loved to talk, so she listened and was surprised to hear of their many former profession. she had never given a thought to why the people were in the nursing home, but just from taking to them on the porch, she came away with a different understanding. Sickness has no boundary; it attacks whomever it pleases: babies, children, judges, and nurses ... whoever you may be.

she decided that she wanted to help these people live out their lives by assisting them in whatever care they needed. They had to give up their homes to live in a nursing facility, and helping them was what she wanted to do. Mom's boss had been watching her and saw how she cared and was attentive in listening to the residents as they talked about what they could no longer do for themselves without help. It was almost summer, and the boss came up to her and asked if she would like a summer job. she told her she would be thankful to get a job. She told her to fill out an application and submit it, and an interview would be set up—her very first. She told her to dress simply but nicely for the interview.

she wore a dark blue dress with black shoes. The interviewer was a pretty young lady, who complimented her outfit and gave her some advice before beginning the interview. She said to her, "You could be sitting here doing this interview." she thought for a second, *What class would she need to take to know the procedure*—but when she offered her the position, she was excited to know she would be earning money for her to live beyond her summer school job experience money became an important thing school was put on the back burner. And earning money by taking care of people in need was more important.

Those conversations opened her eyes to the realization that people in nursing homes had once led active lives. This understanding spurred her to consider with greater awareness the divine purpose for her own life. she realized that sickness is like the rain: it showers or it pours, and it gives no preference to those it consumes. This awareness helped her to better care for her children, instilling love and closeness in them for each other.

Careen, her mom, had succeeded in her determined quest to leave Jamaica and make something of herself in a foreign country; her destination was ordained for her to bring charlotte to the United States, because without her knowing it, she had to get her to the place where God had determined for charlotte to be. And without the restless spirit to drive her she would have not have completed the will and purpose of God in a timely manner. Careen had managed to enroll herself in nursing school and was working as a licensed practical nurse. Her desire had been fulfilled, and the struggle within her spirit had found peace. She had completed her mission as the world standard would have required her to do. Careen suddenly stopped working one day, said she was tired. And never worked again.

her work as nursing assistant was very conscientious and rewarding. When she had gained the apartment, life felt more secure for her and her young family, but she was lacking her own transportation. she had to depend on public transportation.

A neighbor introduced himself and said he had been watching her coming and going. He was concerned that she did not have her own transportation and got home so late at night, walking alone from the bus stop.

One evening that man came to her door. She answered the knock, and he said, "May I come in? I want to talk with you." He said he was the owner of a local car lot and wanted to offer her a car. He showed her the various keys he was carrying. He asked her to choose one and told her that car would be hers.

she was stunned that someone, especially a stranger, would offer her such a gift. Naturally, she was reluctant to accept such an unbelievable offer. she didn't know what his true motives were and couldn't imagine that a man would give a woman such a gift without expecting something from her. He told her that the only condition was that she keep the car clean inside!

By that time in her life, she had experienced several unusual encounters that she attributed to God. she had become somewhat accustomed to entertaining strangers who appeared with unusual petitions. Still, she was wisely cautious with the man, concerned that he would expect her to relinquish herself to him in exchange for his kindness. As it turned out, that was not the case. He was passive and proved to be true to his offer. This amazing encounter—this practical gift from God that met her needs—strengthened her faith that he would always supply all her needs:

> My God will meet all your needs according to the
> riches of his glory in Christ Jesus. (Philippians 4:19)

> Do not forget to show hospitality to strangers, for by
> so doing some people have shown hospitality to angels
> without knowing it. (Hebrews 13:2)

The gift of a vehicle from a stranger was another tangible example to me of how God's road map is not our own. His thoughts and His ways are not ours; they are higher.

> As the heavens are higher than the earth, so are my
> ways higher than your ways and my thoughts than your
> thoughts. (Isaiah 55:9)

Six years passed before her future husband walked into her life—the man she would marry, with whom she would have her third and fourth children. She quickly realize this was not from God but a test in her life, she had asked the Lord previously for a husband, but she had come to realize that He was more concerned about giving her His best in this life and leading her toward His purpose for her. she had grown in Christ but was still striving to look beyond this world and what it has to offer. she considered what Jesus had said to His disciples before He ascended into heaven:

> Do not let your hearts be troubled. You believe in God; believe also in me. My Father's house has many rooms; if that were not so, would I have told you that I am going there to prepare a place for you? And if I go and prepare a place for you, I will come back and take you to be with me that you also may be where I am. (John 14:1–3)

she held on to her faith that He had greater things in store for her than the temporary things this life offers Her husband was a good man. He was a good husband and father. His mom had passed, and a few years later, his father had passed. Our relationship was an unusual one; we found laughter when we should be angry with each other. We were able to talk and hold each other up in conversation. In the end, this was not the husband God had ordained for her life. Still, after we were divorced we remained friends, even to this day.

her dad had continued to visit her once a year in America. When he first saw her, he was very disappointed in the way Careen had not allowed her to excel, instead prompting her toward unreachable goals. He was also disappointed that she had two children. she could see the disappointment in his face. she got the impression from him that her life should have been like Samuel's from the Bible. Samuel's mom had given him to Eli, the priest, who dedicated and raised him unto the Lord—just as her dad had dedicated her life to the Lord just after she was born. Dad believed her mom was spiritual enough or knew enough about God to lead and direct an ordained life, but Careen did not want to have anything to do with God, His church, or His mission. She tried to get rid of her by sending her to live with different family members. She always told her that she was too holy, and she did not like looking on her.

charlotte looked at Careen with compassion and understanding about a nature she herself had not come to understand. she was driven to extend forgiveness and love toward both her parents. Oftentimes in her childhood, she would stand by Dad's side without saying a word. He would look up at her from his seat and say, "What is it?" Charlotte would say, "I love you." He would ask why. There was a knowing deep within her that saw his pain and struggle as he came through that gate day after day and sat in the yard watching her play. It only made her love him for what he could not control.

she saw his pain and knew he did not want to be trapped, but his actions required a reaction. Now he lost his drive to excel and to show his best qualities. So he drank to dull the defeating spirits that reminded him of his potential. He was no longer motivated to reach or achieve He had refused to let someone else's direction and manipulation become their best through him. So he drank and drank, but he was able to find where her home was, and he made it clear when he came through the gates that he was there only to spend time with his daughter. He sat in the yard under a large tree until he was ready to leave then he slipped through the gates. There were no hugs or goodbyes between her and her dad, because he had made it clear that she should not come close to him, because he was a drunk, and he did not want to hurt her. Therefore, we did not say goodbye because he would be back, again and again—until the day he took her to the airport.

Then he came to the united states and saw charlotte once a year after he had gotten his visiting visa, until she said that final goodbye to him. There he sat in the back seat of his brother's car, telling her about his departure. After she got out of the car and stood there looking at him, taking in every bravery he emanated for her, she reached into the car over the door separating us, and she hugged him for a short while. There were no tears, just a knowing that he would not be coming next year.

He had described his final moments to her earlier, in such a ceremonial way that he said, "You won't make it off the plane in time to see the funeral." It was enough for her to have heard it from him. He stood looking up in the clouds for what seemed to be an everlasting memory. Finally as she looked up into the clouds, she saw them swirling in unison she had seen them before as a girl in Jamaica angels of a safe journey.

she was at peace after getting the telegram from his best friend that he had consoled her about his death and getting the news wasn't a shock to her. she called the airport and caught the next flight, but she did not make it in time for the funeral. she felt he knew she was there.

After getting back into the United States, she tried not concentrating on her dad. she could no longer call him up and have those talks we used to have, and he could not say, "Charlotte, the reason for writing is to get a response in writing," and she could not say that in writing she could not hear his voice. Never again would we sit quietly for a minute before starting a conversation again. And he would remind her about the trees and how she climbed up on every limb without fear of falling off. she felt he was sitting there praying that she would not fall. charlotte trusted the tree limbs as her protection. she stayed in the trees because they kept her off the ground where it seemed people hurt and are always in confrontation. In the trees she could fly in her thoughts without hurting because her thoughts was limited.

Her dad would explain about competition, of the love for one thing over the other, and the desire to get rid of the opposition or to cause hurt to the thing that is a hindrance. In these explanations she never questioned him about not spending more time at his home with the children he had there. Whenever he wanted to spend time at his home and desire charlotte company he would take Charlotte to his home, it was on a day he had nothing to do. He would sit on the porch, where he put a chair, and I knew that was my chair, but when I got up to go into the house, he would always come in after a short while and bring me back to the chair.

One of those porch days as she sat with her dad, her little sister came from the house as if a fox had lit fire on her tail. She ran to the gate but did not swing it open but turned her head slowly, without looking at Dad completely. As she proceeded to lift the latch and opened the gate, she eased her body through to the other side. Then she turned her hand to replace the latch and bolted from the gate, not hearing Dad protesting for her to stay in the yard. You would think she was in a marathon race, and the starting gun had sounded.

charlotte turned to Dad and said, "Did you see that?"

He shook his head and said, "I saw that. She left the gate so fast you would think the Germans were coming." That spurred her to catch up with her sister. charlotte got up from the chair just as quickly, but by the time she put her hand on the latch, Dad called her name. she turned to see him pointing to the chair. she looked down the street but saw no trace of her little sister. she walked back to the chair and sat in it.

As a single mother, she worked very hard to keep her family together. She worked the graveyard shift; working through the night was a simpler solution for her and her little family. When the children woke in the morning it was time for them to get ready for school. she had stayed home with her two oldest children; her daughter was six, and her son was five. Before she had started working, her daughter was a little momma for her brother. He relied on her because he was always in trouble, so she was the dependable one who kept the house when charlotte had to work. After school came homework; then their supper was on the table and a little recreation time playing a game or watching their favorite video until it was time for her to get more rest and put them to bed to begin the day in the morning. she always made sure they kept the same schedule on her days off so they were accustomed to the schedule while she worked.

her son knew he should mind the rules of the house while she was away at work and help his sister keep the others entertained with their chores or at playtime. she did not entertain people at home, so her children did not have to be bothered with people coming and knocking on the door. her children are very close. she made sure that they grew up watching out for each other's needs. If one could not tie their shoelace, then the other could teach them how. This concern helped them to stand by each other.

CHAPTER 5

The Gift

At the age of ten, still called Joan instead of Charlotte, moved in with her mom's older sister, who had no children of her own. The Jamaican consulate had denied the first year application. This delayed the schedule for charlott to leave the boarding school and be in the United States with her mom. her aunt was already keeping her oldest and youngest sisters. her aunt knew the procedure of the Jamaican consulate and understood that there would be a required second year of filing for a visa, so when she was asked, she agreed to allow charlotte to live with them.

Her aunt worked at the water district, where she prepared breakfast and lunch for the employees. In fact she cooked two separate lunches, one for the regulars and a second lunch for the officials. She oftentimes took charlotte with her to help serve the lunch and clear empty dishes from the tables.

On days when charlotte did not accompany her aunt to work, charlotte would occupy her time and teach her youngest sister, who was four, how to write and say her ABCs. She was a good learner. Charlotte loved spending time with her little sister, Charlotte father's words rang in her head. That she should read and write with understanding, it will profit her in times to come. When the neighbor's little girl had started school because she was older, charlotte felt that her little sister should be taught how to read and write, so she began to teach her. We did not have extra paper or a slate, but she used the clay earth to teach her to write her ABCs.

When her little sister started kindergarten, she was prepared and knew what to expect going to school, although charlotte was not there to help her with more of her alphabet. she believed her aunt would see her sister through. Our visa had been approved, and we were taken to the airport for departure. Neither our aunt nor our little sister came to the airport, so our goodbyes were made in the yard. We still did not know the concept of goodbye. We were hugging and kissing our families, but until you desire to see one of the family and you realize you have to take the plane to see them, then goodbye has a new meaning.

When we arrived in America, it seemed as if we were stepping into a fictional story. Everything was vastly different in the States from the world we were accustomed to no more climbing trees with smoothe bark and welcome limbs to swing on, no pastures with animals there was air ports airplanes cars trains, you had to be a car owner, to get to unusual places, that was the new world these things became a regular mode of transportation—as different as the spiritual world that had been opened to her sight surrounding the time before she was born into the world and the choices that could be made before entering into one's life in this world.

charlotte could sing that song: ; "The windows of heaven are open, the fire is falling tonight. I've got joy, joy, joy in my heart, since Jesus made everything right. I gave Him my old dirty garment, He gave me a robe of pure white, and now I'm feasting on manna from heaven, and that's why I'm happy tonight."

It's as if the memories she had before she was born had flooded her mind. Everything felt as if it had happened yesterday. charlotte began to recall where she'd been and whom she'd spent the time with. she remembered there was a boy slightly older, and we were always together when we were led into the light from this dark place. she called the caregiver the babysitter; she was huge and broad. Her body looked as if it had no ending, but you could see her design as an individual. She had a neck, but her face was a cloud. When charlotte would cuddle on her chest, she would lift her head to talk with the babysitter, but the face she looked on and talked to was like a cloud.

Our caregiver would allow us to roam outside as you on earth would allow your child to roam, but within the gate or within your sight in the backyard. Our narrow area was flat, and we floated up as the astronauts do when training for low gravity. It was like floating in helium, only there was no air; we were able to breathe but nothing like taking deep breaths. We talked with each other without using words; we had no expression. We just knew it was not to happen because the babysitter said don't do it. My brother, as she called him, always held her hand whenever they were moving around their space. She would always remind him the babysitter said don't go there, but he was always curious as to what was in the area and why we could not look at it.

One day, after the babysitter had brought us out from the dark place and had given us instructions on what we should not do and where we should not go, her brother took her hand and said let's go. He headed right into the area where we'd been told not to go. she kept pulling on his hand, urging him not to go up so far. Then our hands slipped apart, and she went after him. He was up to his waist when she caught up to him. He said look as she looked where he was pointing with his head she saw a city, and there were people there, she tried making out things as she look although she did not know the interpretation of what she was looking at. Then there it caught her attention she heard its voice she look and saw it a swirly black movement it said I will get them if they keep looking, immediately she duck, she was only looking from her chin it set itself to attack she set herself to dodge she tried to get her brothers' attention he was trying to see more then as his attention focus on seeing more, the black swirl threw himself like a snake towards us zooming, she ducked, catching her brother's hand and pulling him down a little, she did not see when the black swirl struck her brother in the chest, then as it lingered then moved away a little. she looked again and saw black smoke swirling about in the distant she ducked again as the swirl look as if it wanted to zoom by us again she did not show her head for a minute. When she looked again, the smoke was making its way back away from her brother.

We could hear the babysitter calling and headed back toward where she was. She was very upset. We did not know what to call her state; we just knew we should not have been there. She took my brother by the hand, never letting go of his hand. It looked as if their hands had become one. She was taking my brother away. He looked at me and said, "You stay right there, I will be back. I will be back," but I never saw my brother again. His words stayed with me; it was a promise she held on to wait, someone is coming. When the babysitter brought her out, she never brought her brother with her. she sat by herself a few more times when the babysitter brought her out; she never questioned the babysitter about her brother. She would only sit where she left her, waiting for him to come so we could go outside.

When we came out from the dark place into the light, our living arrangements were in acrylic-type compartments; they were separated from each other; you could not make contact with the others in their own compartments. In the cubicle next door there was another person by the acrylic fence. He had pressed his body so close to the fence that it looked as if he were one with the fence. she had tried showing her brother that person, but he was only interested in what the babysitter did not want him to be interested in. At first she wondered why this person only stayed on the bottom and was not moving around. Were there others with him who had broken the rule by accelerating up above the great divide and had exposed themselves to a black smoky element that swirl about above us.

We always held hands as we travelled through a helium-filled area (as it seemed) where he went and looked at the forbidden thing and did not yield to my pleas and tugs to get back away from being so close to the great divide. His disobedience or his trial of disobedience was apparently determined by the time we came back in the space of the entrance to the bubble. The babysitter was already standing there, hands on hips, although you could not determine where her hips began and ended. She immediately called him over to her, and she held on to his hand as she made it clear that she was not pleased with him exposing himself to the black element. She kept his hands in hers as she beckoned for charlotte to come closer to her. She took hold of her hand, and we walked into the tube where an acrylic bench was. She released her hand, and she walked to the bench and sat down. The babysitter never released her brother's hand as she continued standing there talking. Then she began walking toward the entrance of the darkness. Her brother said, "Wait for me; I will be back." That was how charlotte life was throughout her junior years and her senior years, waiting for someone to come, just sitting around waiting.

Neither of us knew how serious of an offense it would be to wander near the edge, though the caregiver had told us not to. she was allowed out daily. But she would only sit where her brother had left her, promising her he would be back. But when evening came, the caregiver took her by her hand and led her back through the darkness, Kenneth and Charlotte was not in a state of acclimation we were in a spiritual trial of obedience it is the spirit within us from the beginning that God places in the womb of the mother. Therefore he knows us before we are born on the earth jeremiah 1:5, PSALM 139:16 You are no accident God chose you.

By the third evening, she knew her brother had been sent away. The babysitter never discussed him, nor did she acknowledge that there had been someone who was keeping her company. She knew that wherever he was, there was a place also being prepared for her. Where this place was she cannot tell, but she can remember forcing her eyes to see into the darkness, and all she saw was a bicycle mechanism; then everything became dark. When she was conceived in her mother's womb, it was not to the same womb where her brother had been sent; she was conceived in the womb of a woman whose mind was innovative and whose place of birth was in the Caribbean islands. This place was called Kingston, Jamaica, in the West Indies. This woman was not to be married to a husband who would interfere with the destination of God's plan by not allowing her to travel to the destination where the will of God would be performed.

Charlotte was born through a man who knew of God and the spiritual world—the premortal world—and he understood God's purpose. Therefore he dedicated the newborn child's life back into the care and hands of God, where the will and the purpose of God might become fulfilled through the purpose of why she was born, not in America, to America parents, as her premortal brother, but in a place where His divine power would be executed and His words would ring through: that He knows the number of hairs on your head. But she was born to parents who lived in a country where immigration laws would be a hindrance and the economic condition was not yet developed therefore money was scarce, to pay immigration rates or buy plane tickets. But this was the will of God.

As the years passed and her memory became fulfilled, and she began remembering every detail of her premortal life before she was born, she began thinking of her brother, with the understanding that there were many countries and states, and within these states there were many cities and counties. she did not ponder as to where her brother would be.

she had her experiences through the years of her childhood, traveling from Jamaica to the United States. Through the years of her adulthood, she had children. Once when they were young, she had put them to bed for their naps and felt the need to walk down the stairs from her eighth-floor apartment into the streets. She kept walking; then she felt as if something had begun walking with her. As she began to turn back to her children, the voice assured her the children would be fine, because she would not be gone for a long time. she felt trust and continued walking. Then something else joined them; it was scurrying about and it had a dark appearance. she became frightened and started to run; then the voice said, "If you run, it will run with you," so she did not run. Then she recognized the authority of the voice, and they began talking. At once she asked where her brother was. "This place is large, and you would know just where he is." The voice promised to take her to see him, just as he had promised. He disappeared, so she turned and walked back toward the apartment, where her children were still resting.

Several months turned into years had passed when her sister Karen began dating a young man who had the desire to travel. He asked her to accompany him to Las Vegas, and she went with him, but he became homesick and wanted to come back to Connecticut, closer to his mom. her sister was not so ready to come back; she loved Las Vegas. She called charlotte and invited her to come out there, because her friend was on his way back to Connecticut. He wanted to leave within the next month, so she packed up and traveled to Las Vegas. Charlotte was nineteen, and Karen was twenty-two.

She and her friend visited nightclubs. Some nights charlotte would go with them, but the bartender would not give charlotte any drinks with alcohol; even on her twentieth birthday they still would not give her liquor. she tried hanging out with Karen and her friends, but she heard one of her friends say one night that charlotte was a dead giveaway. she was not sure what they meant, and they asked her to sit at the bar until they had returned. she don't know how long she sat there, drinking one coke after the other.

Then this man came over and asked why she was sitting there. she told him she was waiting on her sister and her friends to return. He said come; he would take you home. she was hesitant and insisted that when her sister returned, she had to be there. He promised that her sister and her friends had left and would not be coming back there for the night. she got up and followed him to his car. she could not believe that Karen would have just driven off and left her in a strange place such as a nightclub.

After getting in his car, he said, "You do not belong in places like that. You should not follow your sister to the club again." He said he came to the club sometimes, and he did not want to see her there again. His voice was stern. she said okay. He said he would walk her to her door and open it for her. she said no and thanked him for taking her home. He said, "I am going to wait here until you go inside, and do not come back out." she said good night and went to bed.

she thought about what the man had said and what Karen's friend had said. she wondered why she was a dead giveaway. What were they doing that if she was with them they would get caught? The man had said she didn't belong in places like bars and clubs; her face stood out in the crowd. she stopped going out with Karen because so much had started happening at the house that she had her hands full trying to understand this new life her sister was living,

Karen asked her to go with her one evening to a hotel, but she wanted charlotte to stand out in the hall. If she did not come out by a certain time, she should knock on the door and insist that she come out. When charlotte knocked, an older gentleman opened the door and insisted that Karen hadn't come in that door. charlotte said she had; she had been standing there waiting on her and needed to see her right now. He opened the door wide to a perfectly spotless room and well-made beds. Then he said to charlotte come in, and she did. He began talking to someone from the other room through a slightly opened door, then he said, "Are you convinced she is not here?" Karen's plans had not worked as she had planned. Someone else's head peeked out from the other room who waved and told the man to let me out of the room.

That was the last time charlotte went on one of Karen's adventures. she began living her own life. Another person had come to join us in Las Vegas, and we spent a lot of time at home or close to home. Charlottes' daughter was at a babysitter. she had found the babysitter through networking, who told her whenever charlotte wanted to go out, just bring her daughter, and she would be safe until she came to pick her up. When she brought her daughter to the sitter, there were several other babies and cribs. They lay in their cribs and were not crying. That was a blessing for her, because Karen's son had been crying for his dad. When Karen's friend left Las Vegas, he had taken him along to his father and his grandmother.

One evening when she came home from work, there was a lot of smoke coming from the apartment. she did not run inside but wondered why no one was standing outside. she walked up to the door and opened it. Everyone was sitting around while Karen was smoking the house with frankincense and myrrh. she asked her what was going on, and she said she was releasing the devil from the apartment. Everyone looked as if they were in a trance. she could not fit herself into this space; everything felt awkward.

All of a sudden the floor got very hot, and the sole of her feet began burning. She started moving about without thinking—she didn't realize what she was doing—but she felt someone walking very close by her footsteps she did not look to see who it was; she was on the move. By the time she was finished moving, she saw her suitcase sitting by the door, packed with all her clothe. she told her sister she was going back to Connecticut. When she bent to pick up her suitcase, there was another beside it. she looked, and her niece had packed her clothes and was ready to say goodbye to her mom and everyone else.

We left and came to Connecticut. she moved in with Careen, and she kept hearing a still small voice saying, "Thursday to Thursday." At first she was skeptical about telling anyone she was hearing voices, but she did not know God outside of knowing Him internally. Then the voice got louder, eventually so loud that she had to lay her head down on the table or the bed to function. The voice sounded as if her head was splitting.

She finally picked up the phone and called her pastor and told her she was hearing voices. She asked, "What is the voice saying?"

Charlotte said, "Thursday to Thursday."

She said, "Hold on," and that's what she was doing when she looked out the window after hearing a car horn. she saw her pastor sitting in her car with the phone in one hand and a jar of water in the other. She said she had been preparing this and did not know who she was preparing it for. She gave charlotte instructions on how to use the water do not drink it because you are hungry, charlotte did not eat anything Wednesday eve by 6pm she was on her knees praying she called Jesus by 9pm she began praying again by 12am she began praying again with hunger coming through she reverse the feeling with intense prayer by 3pm she felt thirsty she prayed and relent to the urge of the thirst she drank a mouth full of water by 6pm she was on her knees praying, by 9 pm she was so weak she rolled off the bed and prayed she stayed on the floor this rhythm charlotte continued by Tuesday she was too weak to wash her face or brush her teeth. She continued the instructions on Wednesday when she pulled herself on her bed from kneeling it was about the 3rd hour in the am when something came over charlotte and the rip happened there was a conversation charlotte could not understand but as if adhesive was being pulled apart she felt free and light by 6pm Wednesday evening she felt light she got up did her personal care and kept praying until Thursday at 6pm she was to drink some chicken broth charlotte had no appetite she felt full she followed her instructions, she was at careens' house she had total control of her grandchildren the children never came into my room or knock on the door and by the following Thursday charlotte was delivered. Something had leaped from her body. she felt the rip by that next Wednesday evening on Thursday she felt like a new person. God brought her mind back, and she saw all that was desired for her if she had not left when God had said to go. Still, it was not an optional choice; the floor had been very hot, and when there was a spot to stand in, it became extremely hot in a few seconds. she praised God for the grace to follow His directions.

she had applied for housing and had gotten it shortly after submitting her credentials during her interview. she moved into the two-bedroom apartment they had given her and her two children. she made living manageable for them; she had a job during the graveyard shift. she did not socialize, so she was able to go to work without anyone knocking on the door and interrupting their home life. she had established a lifestyle before her children and herself and completed it by becoming a faithful member of the church.

Several young people about her age attended Bible way Church of God in Christ Jesus. They were young mothers trying to live a life unto the Lord. The pastor had tarry and prayer night on Tuesday night, and we showed up with our little ones; they would fall asleep on the pews as we tarried for the Holy Ghost.

Convocation week soon came, and we had to drive to Greensville, North Carolina. Usually the pastor herself and another car would travel together. On this trip, her car was the one being used. It was excellent for the road trip going and coming, but it had no steering bolts, and we could not wait another day to get the bolts on the car. We prayed and took off on our travels.

As we approached the Greenville freeway, there was no traffic. The evangelist who was traveling with her and her two children took turns with her at the wheel. she had been driving, and we had decided to switch drivers, but the sun had begun to rise and was shining so brightly that sleep could not be held back. charlotte never fall asleep when traveling on the road, whether she was driving or not, but her eyes got heavy and she drifted off. When she had awoken several minutes later, she looked at the evangelist; she was asleep, and so were charlotte children in the back seat.

she turned her attention to the road. We were driving in the center of the road, not swerving but in one straight line charlotte sat and watch the miracle for awhile. she watched for another moment and then said something, and the evangelist opened her eyes. A car was approaching in the far distance, and we needed to keep to our side of the street. Soon we had brought the car in line properly on the right lane.

The pastor had already reached the hotel and was getting registration in order by the time we pulled up. We went to our rooms refreshed and got ready for the day service. We were in church the remainder of the evening and into the night. Her children were exhausted, so she left the night service a little early to give them something to eat and put them to bed before the evangelist got to the room. The children fell asleep almost before lying down. charlotte got on her knees and began praying after tidying up her side of the room, and then crawled into bed.

A little later the evangelist put her key in the door and came into the room. she heard her when she began to pray, charlotte rolled out of bed and onto her knees and began to pray along with the evangelist. Suddenly the Holy Ghost came into the room, and she began to speak in a tongue she had never spoken before. It was so slippery, then a light shone and she began speaking in a tongue so light and pure she spoke for half a second in this language then the light trailed away and another language began coming from her mouth, she have not spoken in that language since that day. she knew that she was filled with a heavenly language, but she also knew she had spoken in a language not designed for everyday use; it was airy and light.

During this time Karen and charlotte had been separated, although we lived in the same state. Karen showed up at charlotte home with a son, and she was pregnant with twins. As she questioned her as to who her children's father was, she surprised her by asking, "Who does her son resemble?"

This reminded charlotte of the story of the Sphinx, a mythical creature who sat in front of Thebes and posed a riddle to everyone passing by. If you could answer it the sphinx let you go. Those who could not answer its riddle suffered a fate. She was surprised to learn she would cross such barrier, but she did, and there were three proofs to the fact. Along with a license or certificate of marriage, charlotte was pleased at Karen's gracious achievement and her beautiful nephews.

During the separation, she could not share whom she had encountered and what she had done with her life, but her mystical experiences were mysterious to her and would only make Karen skeptical. she had been off living in her world without Christ. This was a painful thing, as memories always plague you when the spirit of righteousness is upon you and is a presence in your everyday walk of life he is leading and guiding you. The Lord had brought Karen back into her life. She now had four children, having defeated all odds. She was told she would have no children; then she had a gorgeous daughter, and now she had gotten married and had her three boys.

Charlotte was very happy for her. She no longer talked about not knowing whom she should become or what she should reject or accept. she was in the church, and Karen had read the Bible. She had a pastor and a church she attended in Bridgeport, Connecticut. Charlotte would oftentimes leave her church and attend functions at Karen's church. There was always a tent service, so on this particular Sunday after coming from church, the Lord said, "Go here." she asked where, and He began to lead. If you follow, then you will arrive where He desires for you to go.

she had reached the house of her mother-in-law. They were just gathering to have prayer. Her mother-in-law invited her to join them in prayer. As she sat down and we held hands and they began chanting, she did not get to say a word. The Holy Spirit whisked her away, and we went on a journey. We were walking, and as I looked around, I could see people kneeling on the ground. We walked further and came to a wall. We went across it and found more people kneeling. We kept walking and came to another wall and went across it. There were a few more people on this side than there were in the middle.

We kept walking and came to a third wall. The Spirit stopped over this person kneeling and digging up the dirt. she asked who this person was. The spirit walked her around in front of the person, and as the person lifted her head and she saw her face, the Spirit said, "I am going to take her spirit out from her."

charlotte began to ask the Lord if she could get some time to reason with Karen; maybe there was a chance, and she would realize her error and ask for forgiveness. But Karen was too far gone. After seeing her in this vision, one day as we was driving, charlotte spoke to her and told her what the Lord had showed her. She looked at charlotte and said she knew He would be mad at her, but she couldn't help herself. charlotte fell apart while driving as she tried to explain to Karen, "This is the man who owns the breath you are breathing, and He wants retribution, and all you can say is you can't help yourself. What have you done?" As she traveled with her, she began to see her mystical powers not in the secular world but in the church, upon people who trust and depend on the Lord as their backbone. "Of course he is going to take you off the earth. You have crossed boundaries, and the blood of these His people is crying out to Him to deliver them."

she made it her purpose to hang out with Karen, and as they walked one day on the west side of the town in Connecticut where we lived, Karen said she had gotten her diploma. charlotte was excited for her and began praising her, but she pointed to a building and said, "There is a school in that building, and that's where I got my diploma."

charlotte knew of the building and stood still looking at Karen for a while. "What school is in that building?" She said it was a school for witches. she was disappointed and began to reflect on the quiet voice she had been listening to through her childhood as the spirit of Karen's father.

It was something Karen struggled with. She was defeated because she could not identify its character and make amends despite her inner turmoil, and reject its wants and desires from developing. She could not identify her feelings of struggle. She knew there was a presence driving her that had much more power and strength than she had. She had no reflection looking back at her and her inquiry. She went for what was unknown, not heeding the calm still voices that forbade her. Through it all trust in Jesus.

I saw the struggle within karen, and as we lived separate lives, she became a victim to the weak and beggarly elements. Through Karen's struggle and disobedience to the Lord, He had decided that Karen and charlotte could no longer unite or live in the same state as they once had. She had to leave Karen's world. The Spirit came to her and asked where in the world she would like to travel. she said Las Vegas, knowing she would be able to get a job as soon as she got there. she had her credentials and knew how to renew them if they needed renewal.

she packed up her things and her children and headed back to Las Vegas as a new person looking at life differently. After settling in our apartment and getting her children in school, she headed out the next day in search of a job in the places she knew she could get employment. And yes, she started working at Sunrise Hospital through the agency.

The New Year had come, and as she was at home, her phone rang. It was Karen telling her what she was about to do. charlotte tried talking her out of her plan, and as charlotte turned her head partially into the room still talking with Karen, she saw a puff of smoke. charlotte sniffed and did not smell smoke from cooking. she sniffed again and did not pick up any fumes. she got up and walked into the kitchen; nothing was cooking, and the stove was not turned on.

she walked back into the bedroom and sat on the bed by the window. When she turned her head toward the window, she could see outside. When she turned to look inside the apartment, again she saw the smoke. There in the midst of the smoke, a disco club appeared. There were people moving about. Then a taxi pulled up to the club, and the date who had invited her sisters and her cousin to the club extended his arm as the taxi door opened. He did not walk up to the taxi; he extended his arm from inside the club, and he helped her sister out of the taxi. She and those with her went into the club, where they sat at a table, they ordered drinks, and took a sip of their drinks.

Then as they got up to go on the dance floor, charlotte saw a hand pass over one of the bottles and release something into it. she knew this was not a good meeting, nor was this the group she wanted to be in company with. she tried warning her sister, as she oftentimes would let her know of dangers. This time the spirit would not allow charlotte to tell anything to her sister. Like Jeremiah when he could not show his joy by helping his wife choose a baby's name for their son until the child was born, so she had become dumb. As she tried to talk, she sounded like a mute person trying to speak. The only encouragement that came from charlotte lips that made sense was "Go to church"; that is what you should be doing. It was the New Year, and that was what we would have done.

"Charlotte," she said, "then come so we can go to church." But Charlotte knew she could not just get on a plane and go. They ended the conversation with her going to the club.

While living in Las Vegas she had found a Church of God in Christ Jesus after consulting Google to find a church to attend. she became a member and was very active. she was the YPWW leader, and they had wonderful services. The pastor conducted many revivals.

One revival he had was one he called A Long Time Coming. The title caught charlotte attention, and she had decided she would not miss this revival. She was a little late getting to her seat, but as soon as she walked in and saw the guest speaker, she knew he was her premortal brother.

There were so many voices in her head that night—*Does he remember you? Will he give you a hug?*—but this one voice said, "Think" "You have lived separate lives and had many difficulties". "Be strong." All she wanted was for her brother to remember her and at least give her a hug. But the voice she never forgot is the one that said, "He is different; he's had a lot of experiences, just like you."

All she wanted was her brother. She had waited like he said, and she wanted to hear hello, how are you? With a hug. she was crushed. "He is different now" was all she could repeat. she expected a hug or a hello. After she got home, she went in her room and cried like a baby; for a whole week she cried. Every chance she got she stole away by herself and let it pour, she had waited for him, and when she saw him, he walked by as seeing she was a stranger.

God made her cry until she had exhausted and was finished. Then He said, "Your understanding is different from the understanding he has. You had been brought up differently." Her understanding was that her memory was refreshed completely; his memory was probably vague until he heard her say he looked different in the flesh (and likely still vague after that). It was seeing him on the pulpit when she recognize the blackened area in his chest, she immediately understood why he had to be separated from her but also that's when she knew the swirly creature had stung him and the baby sitter had separated us immediately. charlotte was able to identify him without a doubt by his blackened chest

Through this experience, God had further proved to her that He is faithful to His promise and that He knows us before we are born and carries us through life on earth in the direction of His will.

> You created my inmost being;
>> you knit me together in my mother's womb.
> I praise you because I am fearfully made;
>> your works are wonderful,
>> I know that full well.
> My frame was not hidden from you
>> when I was made in the secret place,
>> when I was woven together in the depths of the earth.
> Your eyes saw my unformed body;
>> all the days ordained for me were written in your book
>> before one of them came to be.
> How precious to me are your thoughts, God!
>> How vast is the sum of them!
> Were I to count them,
>> they would outnumber the grains of sand
>> —when I awake, I am still with you. (Psalm 139:13–18)

If only we would put our complete trust in God, believe in Jesus, listen for the voice of God's Holy Spirit, and walk in obedience to His divine direction.

CHAPTER 6

Karen

Karen was a pretty baby. She had light skin and brown fine hair. She was not blessed with the shapely physique of her mother, but she had the beauty of proportion—a nose to fit her face, thin lips ... it all came together to give her that Imani look,

She cried a lot when she was a baby until her mother took her to the doctors, to find out why her pretty baby cried often. That's when the doctors ran tests and told her mom that she had sickle cell anemia, a disease where there aren't enough healthy blood cells to carry adequate oxygen throughout the body. This came from one parent having the recessive gene and the other parent the dominant one, which resulted in an inherited group of disordered blood cells that had a sickle shape. This news was devastating to her mom; she gave up a lot of her lifestyle and stayed home with her sick baby. Karen grew up cuddled; she was always offered someone's lap or getting a hug.

As Karen grew, she grew close with Charlotte She found she could tell her things and did not have to hear about them from anyone else. She always shared with charlotte, her deepest darkest thoughts. She went with her mom to most places, and she would confide in charlotte about the things she saw there.

Karen hated the dark collage of feelings that always encased her like a heavy storm cloud on the verge of a downpour. The war inside her made for a constant uncertainty about who she was, who her dad was, and whether or not he even loved her or thought about her or even cared for her at all.

She carried questions and uncertainties about what was truth in her life and what was not and uncertainties about what she should accept and reject about her dad that might ease her burdened spirit and bring peace and an identity to her life. charlotte could not convince her to look within and find for herself what she wanted to become, because there was such a turmoil within.

What she wanted was identification, but another dark part of her also wanted to be present, and what she chose would be the ultimate choice. She was at a point of discovery in her life, to let go and let something persuade her thoughts. In order for a new beginning to occur, she had to entertain a change from the struggle you cannot seem to refuse. Only God can bring about that change, for He alone knows the struggle within, and His redemptive, transforming power can change those who seek after His help and healing.

Karen did not seek the one who has all the answers, because she was not brought to the one who could heal all diseases. Although she saw her sister leaving the house for church, she never dressed up and went along with her. Therefore Karen struggled with finding her identity. She was exposed to so many other healing powers that she could not bring herself to say God is the ultimate healer.

> My dear friends, as you have always obeyed—not only in my presence, but now much more in my absence— continue to work out your salvation with fear and trembling [deep reverence for God] …. (Philippians 2:12)

Nevertheless, charlotte felt responsible for Karen's pain. Although her mom had four other children, God had a purpose why only Karen and she had such a special bond and were raised together yet separate from childhood.

When we arrived in the United States, the Lord had a heart-to-heart talk with charlotte. He said, "You are not under the watchful eyes of your dad. Here is what I want you to do: I do not want you to follow after divination or mediums or anything to do with drinking of blood. Keep away from those who practice witchcraft, and do not read the palm. You are gifted, but your gift is for the use of the Lord. Do not tell fortunes." she held strongly to these admonitions from the Lord and to His word.

Karen often said, "Why am I not gifted as you are? Why can you tell of so many things and I can't?" she would explain to her that the gift came from God, and if she desired to have the gift, she should ask God, and He would give it to her. Karen had not had the spiritual encounter with the Holy Ghost that she had experienced; she only knew charlotte had something she wanted, and she did not want to ask God for it. She could not be persuaded to turn to God wholly.

The difference between us two sisters was like oil and water, especially the way we each approached life and responded to circumstances and relationships. Karen had gotten a new job and had asked charlotte out to lunch to celebrate her new job. She told her where to meet her. It was a redeveloped building in town, and Karen had gotten the receptionist position. charlotte rode the escalator to the top floor, where karen looked beautiful sitting at her glass desk with the different phone lines. I stood and admired her for a moment until it was time for her to take her lunch break. charlotte asked why she was sitting out in the hall on top of the stairs. Shouldn't the receptionist area be a little more formal? It looked like a drop-by where visitors were not invited to sit for long. She said something offhanded; regardless, charlotte was happy for her and celebrated her new job.

To help build Karen's low view of herself, charlotte always made a point to praise her achievements and compliment her whenever she had done a good job. she was also honest with her whenever she saw Karen making poor choices and needing to make some sort of change. Despite these efforts to show authentic love to her sister, Karen would rebel. She would say to her compliments and advice, "Stop it, Charlotte."

After church one Sunday, charlotte was looking forward to getting home and stretching out. she had worked a difficult week. As she changed out of her church clothes, the Lord's Spirit approached her and made it be known to her that He would remove Karen from the earth. It was a devastating revelation. The Lord had prepared for her a place where He would be able to show her why He had made the decision about Karen. she felt the urge to leave the house but was not sure where to go. After getting in the car, she started toward Karen's home but was turned around by discouragement. She drove to the south of the city in the vicinity of her ex-mother-in-law's house and felt the need to knock on their door. Her ex-mother-in-law came to the door and invited her in. She said they were about to have prayer and asked if she would like to join them, she said okay.

We got in a circle and held hands. As they began to chant, she listened. Then, as she opened her mouth to say "Jesus," the Spirit took her away. At first we walked in silence; He was leading her then it seem like a cemetery in the spirit we walk and her mind could not believe where she thought she was. Then she began to recognize the area. We had walked into a graveyard and walk through the first section then we came upon a wall, but we continued past it There were several people in the first part, we walked through the wall, we continue walking in the spirit. We came to a second area of the graveyard there were a few people not as many as in the first we continued in the spirit walking and upon a second wall and kept walking through. Not far ahead, in the third section there was not that many people but she did recognize the few that was there, they walked until she could see a third wall and a woman kneeling in the dirt of the graveyard with her back to us. When we got to her, we stood behind her for a few minutes. she said to the Lord who is this, Charlotte was not able to see her face until we walked around and stood in front of the kneeling woman. She raised her head, and charlotte saw that she was her sister Karen. There the Lord repeated to her that He would be taking Karen from the earth. "I am taking the spirit out of her" He said,

I was deeply stricken with grief, there in my ex-mother-in-law's house, in the circle of prayer. It was a circle of love and security and understanding God's judgment. I could not contain my emotions; my grief spilled out, and I sobbed uncontrollable. The prayer group quickly formed a circle around me, holding hands and praying, not knowing why such grief had taken hold upon me or why I was thrashing about. My former mother-in-law entered the circle, held me tightly, and asked, "What happened?"

I could only say, "God is going to kill her!"

She tried comforting charlotte by reminding her of the story of Hezekiah from 2 Kings 20. He was very ill, and the prophet Isaiah told him that God was going to take his life. Then Hezekiah prayed and God told Isaiah that He would extend Hezekiah's life by fifteen years.

The story did not encourage charlotte. Karen was by the third wall what was on the other side charlotte felt no comfort or peace that God would grant mercy to Karen and spare her life. she was still engaged in the graveyard vision. she walked with the Spirit of God toward the third wall, but He did not reveal what was behind the wall. I asked Him to spare Karen's life but heard no response. Then charlotte felt His Spirit melt away with the fading vision. she made several attempts to persuade Karen that God had determined her stay on earth and that she must repent and turn she said she could not. However, Karen was too far-gone

A year later Karen grew ill. God had extended her life but she had not repented. She continued her mission as her will commanded her to perform. charlotte had no strength to visit Karen, this sickle cell episode was as unusual as the cup of sugar they said was on the counter then disappear, when she went into the hospital, although she thought of her daily. Believing Karen's illness this time was a result of God's anger toward Karen's choices against Him, charlotte waited on the Lord's direction.

> Those who wait on the Lord
> Shall renew their strength;
> They shall mount up with wings like eagles,
> They shall run and not be weary,
> They shall walk and not faint. (Isaiah 40:31 NKJV)

One sunny afternoon, she began getting dressed. she had no particular place in mind to go, but it was as if she had someplace to go. Hot sunny days in Connecticut can be humid, we have the cove and the sea breeze which brings in the hot air across the city with a cent of ocean air you can't be angry with the humidity As she continued getting dressed, a knock came at the door. she was surprised to see her cousin standing there. she invited her in, and as we began to talk, she finished getting dressed. Then her cousin said, "Let's go driving." We got into the car and began driving with no destination in mind. We soon found ourselves in the area of the hospital. We parked in the lot and began walking towards the hospital entrance. The receptionist looked up and greeted us as we greeted her in return and continued walking toward the elevator. she punched the familiar number two button, and we emerged on that floor. At the nurses' station, she stopped to ask where her sister's room was. It seemed that God had appointed this time for her to visit her sister.

Her cousin walked ahead of she after hearing the room number she walked toward Karen's room. When she saw the room number, she turned right into the room. As charlotte walked up to the door, she immediately saw activity that was not visible to the natural eyes. she stopped at the door, looking around at several gathered figures. Someone bolted from the room as she began observing them, and then she remembered her cousin. She looked toward the side of the room where her cousin had pressed her body to the wall aiming for the closest chair, there she was trying to get to a chair she saw. When she finally reached it, she sat down as if she had ended a long journey and needed a chair.

The activity in the room brought her attention back to the other side of the room. Of several people there, she knew some of them, but what was astonishing was the man directing the activity. He stood at the head of Karen's bed as if holding a door open; then he began telling everyone they had to leave the room. They began leaving through the door in the wall near where he stood, one by one. The two ladies kneeling at the foot of the bed were the last to leave. The glasses one lady was wearing made me remember her clearly, along with several others.

After the last two had left the room, the man in charge looked around the room before he disappeared into the wall door, and the area became a wall once again. Then Karen turned her head to me and said, "I thought you were never coming."

This confirmed to the realization that without God I can do nothing; without God I would fail. I said to her, "Without God, your life is helpless. You need God for the strength you use daily."

she was still standing at the door; the Spirit had not given her clearance to enter the room. Then the Spirit spoke and said, "This is the moment you asked Me for. Now pray."

she prayed the prayer, "Death, get back," as if it was the last prayer. The surrounding hospital floor was utterly still and quiet after the prayer. Then a nurse showed up to give the patient in the next bed her medication, and normal activity resumed. It is always a marvel to experience God's activity in spiritual duel.

If only she had asked God to forgive her and abstained from her doings, God would have extended her life, as he did for Hezekiah. But she insisted she had no control of what was happening, even thou she knew her faith that God would not be pleased with her choice she made a choice defying the words that was spoken to her as she washed sheets in the back yard on Anderson road in 1968 that she would anger God.

Several months earlier before leaving Connecticut, Karen had introduce me to a young man, she said he was brought to her from another state and they had become close, but a disagreement had aroused as to exactly who the wanderer were suppose to be close with, she introduce him as a friend of a cousin.

Charlotte already knew the Lord was getting ready to take Karen's life, she did not know what role the young man might be playing, so she did not eat the food he brought. Now here he was again. The man who had directed the scene in Karen's hospital room was the same man who had stretched his hand from inside the club to the outside to assist Karen and the others from the taxi. He was also the same one who came to her sister's house after the funeral and went with her to buy Kentucky Fried Chicken. When he asked her what she was having, she could not relinquish her knowledge and be overcome by hunger. she was not hungry and bought enough food for the others; he wanted to know why she was being standoffish.

Karen was the sibling who seemed to need the most spiritual guidance and protection. But even if charlotte purpose in life was to aid others to the extent that she was able without enabling poor choices, she knew this purpose included her sister, though it would be Karen's choice alone to accept her help. It was never clear to her when or how she was to provide spiritual intervention for her sister beyond prayer; nor did she know when and how she was to separate herself to avoid interfering with God's divine work in Karen. Therefore it was a tedious line she was always striving to balance.

From an early age, she had known inside (just as her dad had) that she was born with a distinctive purpose, and she believed that Karen had been born with a unique purpose too. Nevertheless, Karen could not grasp hold of that belief for herself and give it back to God. she knew that no one but Karen could choose that she should know Jesus as her Savior and find God's destiny for her life. Karen recognized that she need welcomed

Jesus and be more deeply rooted in her belief that Christ is the only one who is able to divinely calm life's storms, heal wounds, and fill voids. Karen rejected these beliefs; she did not understand why God chose her to suffer, and for this, somehow, she held a bitter resentment in her heart and would not release its sting.

Karen and charlotte were different in character. Karen loved to put on makeup and wear a fur coat over a pair of hot pants. charlotte preferred to wear a suit with an attaché case. People often commented that she presented herself as someone white, and her sister acted as though she were black. When she heard these comments charlotte believed there was an exchange in identity, because Karen hated who she was, and charlotte wanted her to be comfortable in her skin. When exactly this change had come about, neither of us could say; we just took on each other's role and began living happily.

In all her years in Jamaica, she never once thought differently about Karen- or others, especially those in her family who also had the same color skin as Karen. she had grown up in a family of diversity, so it never occurred to her that the color of one's skin was an issue—until she came to live in the United States. Jamaica was predominantly black and had a minority of Asian and Caucasian, but even in interacting with people of different colors, it never occurred to her to dislike someone because of their skin color. Faced with such prejudice in the States, she discovered an edge in many white people that she rarely saw in black people. In such times she would go to God and ask, "Why are people so against each other because of skin color? Moreover, why do she not have that edge-that prejudice-with those of a different color?"

God answered, saying she had been preordained and would go to different nations, telling them, "Thus says the Lord," and there must be no barrier between her, His Word, and His people. Even though she did not understand His sayings at the time, she believed the word she heard coming to her and knew God would make His meaning clear.

> Jesus appeared to the Eleven as they were eating; he rebuked them for their lack of faith and their stubborn refusal to believe those who had seen him after He had risen.

He said to them, "Go into all the world and preach the
gospel to all creation. Whoever believes and is baptized
will be saved, but whoever does not believe will be
condemned." (Mark 16:14–16)

As an adult she eventually chose to immerse herself in the Word of
God, Bible studies, worship, and prayer with other believers in Christ. She
came to believe with all her heart that Jesus is the only way to God the
Father and that He sent Jesus—His one and only Son—to earth in human
form to pay the final penalty for all of mankind's sins. she believe He made
this incomprehensible sacrifice because of His great and unconditional
love for every human being, His divine creation. Moreover, she believe
the Word of God, that nothing can separate her, Karen, or anyone from
the love of God.

For I am convinced that neither death nor life, neither
angels nor demons, neither the present nor the future, nor
any powers, neither height nor depth, nor anything else
in all creation, will be able to separate us from the love of
God that is in Christ Jesus our Lord. (Romans 8:38–39)

Once as she shared time with Karen, strolling through a familiar
section of town, she told her that she had gotten her high school diploma.
Charlotte was ecstatic and started giving her kisses on the cheeks. Then
she wanted to know at which college she was getting ready to pursue her
studies. She withdrew herself and said it was not a regular high school
diploma, so she said, "How can you get into college if you don't have a
high school diploma?"

She said, "Oh! I went to a school, but it was not a regular school. It was
in that building over there." She pointed toward a familiar place frequented
by some of my acquaintances who had told me to wait for them while they
went inside. When they came back, they told me the person inside said
never to bring me inside when they visited. she had tried to get information
about that building, but the conversation got diverted and she would not
pursue the information. Until that day. Karen told her that building was

a house where witches were trained, and when you had qualified, you got a diploma.

she was in such shock that she stood there with her mouth open, reflecting on the lives she saw changed before her eyes because they chose to excel in Dante's world of the *Inferno*, which tells the journey of Dante through hell guided by the ancient Roman poet Virgil. Hell is depicted as nine circles of suffering located within the Earth. This is the realm of those who have rejected spiritual values by yielding to bestial appetites or violence or by perverting their human intellect to fraud or malice against their fellows.

Karen has sold her soul was all she could say to herself as she stood there. This voice came to her, saying, "Save her now. She got away from you and did what she wanted, something you would have prevented if she had told you her whereabouts, so she stayed away." she was at a loss. charlotte could not save her; she had made her decision to rebel against God. she was stunned and did not know what to say. she asked Karen if she thought about going to church. Karen said she was in church, and her church was in Bridgeport. charlotte said she would come with her one Sunday.

We showed up at Karen's church, and when church began, the pastor's wife came out to the pulpit dressed in a little shroud. I said to Karen, "Why would she wear that outfit? It seems as if it got put in the dryer with a towel, and the fuzz from the towel is all over the outfit." Karen's reply floored me. After hearing and seeing Karen's new power and strength, she knew she had to say something. she immediately turned to Karen and told her she could not under any circumstance harm God's people. There were many other instances when God had me witness of Karen's demise to His people. Then she started going to her own church, leaving Karen in her church.

One weeknight Karen's church was holding a tent revival and she was dressed to attend. she told Karen she felt uncomfortable sitting in the rear of the church. "she will sit in the middle, but not the back." This night Karen insisted she and her would sit in the back.

She sat there with her for a while but became uncomfortable. she moved up to the middle of the tent, and Karen reluctantly came and sat with charlotte. She said, "Charlotte, she was too close. she can't sit this close to the pulpit." As she was trying to understand her, we were all staring straight ahead as the devotional singers were about to start devotional service. It was as if something counted one, two, three, and we all turned to look toward the street because that was where the Spirit had tossed Karen from the center of the tent.

Awestruck, she ran into the street after Karen. She said, "I told you I was too close to the front. Now we have to go." She wanted to stay but had not driven her own car. she wanted to stay and hear the service but did not want to cause any harm. The pastor knew Karen had stepped way over her head into wrath. We went looking for the car, and we found it and left.

On the way she explained to Karen how the Lord was not pleased with her choices and was angry with her. She turned to face her and said, "she knew He would be mad at her, but she can't help herself." And with everything she knew, she felt at a loss. she did not know how to begin to bring someone back from the entrance of hell, especially since the Lord had already declared she was no longer to stay on the earth.

Karen had a liking for the unknown, the dark side of our world, a liking that she kept as a secret to herself because of her illness. She would travel to places with their mom that she would never have seen. There were secrets that she would come back and reveal to her of things she had seen or heard. Karen knew her secrets were safe with charlotte; she knew she would never reveal them to anyone. she would observe Karen's attitude toward certain family members and could only imagine what her bodily language meant as she expressed her inward feelings without saying a word.

Karen held back most of her secrets until after she had left high school. We drifted apart, though still living in the same city. When we reunited, she was married and had three children—a set of twins and her older child, whom she had right after leaving high school. She came to charlotte home, and we played the guessing game of who was the husband. We went to high school in that city. She had the personality of her mom; she was not afraid of cowboys and their toys. How little was her mind to have ever guess the notorious prince. *But how?* was all she could think. First you had to enter the arena, then you had to cross the domain, then you had to cover over with a sheet. How was all she could ask herself, staring at all the memories. Then she asked her, "Married?" Then the word slipped off her tongue: "How?"

she had her son and had just gotten back from the hospital, as memory pressed her, when Karen rushed in the door. "Come with me," she insisted.

"Where?" she asked.

"I am going to this lady's house down the street." she was in pain. she must have caught a cold in half of my face. The doctor had given her some barbiturates; she took one and decided to walk with karen. We came to this house, and she led the way up the steps and knocked on the door. A woman opened the door and said something to her sister. Almost simultaneously they asked charlotte to sit and wait. she sat for a few seconds; then her sister came walking out from the back room and said, "Let's go," in a hurry. She did not know what to think until the lady came to the door her sister and her had just walked through a few minutes earlier. She leaned on the doorpost looking exhausted.

Her sister hurried her through the front door and onto the sidewalk. After we had walked about half a block, she felt entitled to speak. She also wanted to look behind, but her sister held her close to her body and encouraged her not to look back. Finally she asked her what had happened. She said the woman became epileptic and wanted her out of their house. She ordered her sister to get her out and away from their house. She said the woman could not penetrate charlotte spirit. There was a bright light, and she said she was too powerful to be in their house.

These are some of the acts of her sister as she became more independent within herself. She was drawn to the underworld, and charlotte was an impediment to her research. charlotte had become endowed in the holiness church with much praying and fasting; her mind and spirit were occupied with her family and the church. When her sister showed up at her house, she could not remember what made us separate. she could not understand how we drifted apart and stayed away from each other, living our lives without a phone call in the same city.

she was perplexed until her sister asked her about a house on the hill. she remember she had a girlfriend who visited that house frequently. She would always ask her to stay at the gate on the side walk. She said the sisters who lived in the house did not want her inside. Years after our friendship had dissolved her sister told her about her diploma. She said the house was a school and a church, and she had graduated from their school as a certified witch. she could not contain herself or believe what was being said to her ears. As she put the pieces together, she remembered her girlfriend and the other pieces she told her. It was a concrete confirmation of who those people were. she somewhat understood how the distance was created.

The voice spoke to her that night in her room telling her about the things she should not involve herself with such as fortune-telling or contact with the world of spirits that do not worship the Lord as savior.

Talking with her sister, she received a greater understanding of the veil. The life that we live without God's direction leads us into a lifespan of unforeseen shadows that imitate the natural view of destiny. And human life can intervene in such a way as to hinder or modify our directions.

she watched her sister struggle within herself. It was as if she was struggling in the theory of vector spaces. She found herself being less linear dependent and being linear independent. All I can think is, *Without God, what can one be?* God is not against race crossing, but without God's direction there are consequences. Matt:7,15,16 The enemy comes as a sheep but when he unveils he is a ravenous wolf. Psalm 100:3 Know that the LORD IS God. It is He made us and not we our selves.

charlotte was devastated that Karen did not consider the extent of damage she had brought upon herself by turning against God and toward Satan. You cannot live outside God's protection and His desire for your life. After she asked God to give Karen another chance to make amendment to him for her life, her only spoken words were "I know He would be mad." The choice was Karen's alone to make. The man who owns the breath you breathe has spoken and yet has heard charlotte petition to give you space to ask for mercy and repentance. No one else can say, "I repent," but the soul that wants forgiveness.

> The Lord is not slow in keeping his promise, as some understand slowness. Instead he is patient with you, not wanting anyone to perish, but everyone to come to repentance. (2 Peter 3:9)

CHAPTER 7

Blind Faith

Several weeks later, when the Spirit of the Lord again spoke to her, He simply said, "I am separating you from your sister. You will have to leave her."

she considered where she might go and concluded that the best place would be Las Vegas, where Karen and her had lived in the 1970s. she had connections there and believed she could secure a job shortly after arriving. As she made the necessary arrangements to travel with her four children and their three Cabbage Patch Kids, she felt the presence of the Lord. she thought about His instructions to separate from Karen and remembered how the apostle Paul separated from Barnabas due to their unresolved quarreling (Acts 15:36–39). She was not quarreling with her sister, but Karen had unresolved issues with God and was in denial of how angry He was with her estranged behavior. charlotte have faith in God and believed without doubting that he would take care of her and her family's needs.

Before she left, she once again had a conversation with Karen. This time she told her that God wanted her to move to a different state so that we would no longer be so close and meet each other so frequently. Karen kept to her denial and believed she could not make any changes toward making amends with the Lord.

she had not kept in touch with the people she knew when she left Las Vegas, so this move back was like being in Vegas for the first time. she arrived at the bus station with four children and nowhere to go. she got the newspaper and began looking for an apartment. Seeing rooms for rent, she called, and the lady said she had rooms available, but they were for men only. she explained to the lady that she had just gotten off the Greyhound bus with four children and needed to rent somewhere. The woman said, "Let me talk with my husband." A few moments later she got back on the phone and said her husband would come to get her and her kids from the greyhound bus depot.

Her husband arrived in fifteen minutes and drove them to his home. He and his wife settled them in a vacant two-bedroom apartment. It was not quite physically ready to be rented they said, Charlotte could not find anything that made the apartment not ready to be rented except it needed her furniture but God had made miraculous provision for her and the children to allow this couple to hold the apartment believing the apartment was not ready to be rented this was a blessing and a miracle of God for Charlotte and her children. The couple had not shut off the electricity and continued to pay the bill for the apartment until she could make arrangements with the light company to transfer the service to her name at the end of the month

In search of a school for her children, she gained information from the next-door neighbor, who had school-age children. The mother told her where the school was, and the children and her headed there so they could be registered to attend school. she felt relieved and grateful to God for His great provision over her and her family as she simply walked in faith and obedience to the Spirit of God.

After getting the children registered for school, she still had enough money to pay rent for two months. her next adventure would be to find work. she pulled from memory her employment directory and set off in faith to be placed on someone's payroll. A temporary agency was always good for earning the next tank of gas, but she had the connections and current credentials to land employment for longer than a few days.

she began work immediately in a Las Vegas hospital. There was a demand in the city for hospital workers. It is the custom of Las Vegas to entertain many visitors—tourists who came either by plane or by tour bus to visit the casinos. Many times visitors became ill and had lengthy stays in the hospital, creating a demand for workers.

she recalled the 1970s when her and a friend would sit on top of the hill on Tara Avenue in the evenings after work, watching the lights on the entire strip. We talked about the changes that were being made and how quickly the city was being developed. We sat and talked until the sprinklers came on, soaking the lawn and also us, because we didn't move quickly enough. Then we would turn in to our own house. She had turned twenty-one and frequented a bar that had a pool table in the recreation side. she often played pool games with the customers who wanted to be challenged. They would order drinks and the bartender, whom she did not know personally, would make sure the number of drinks that came into the recreation area matched the number of regular drinkers there. He knew she was twenty and that her birthday was coming up shortly; yet he still refused to let anyone buy her drinks. Even after she showed him her license with her age as twenty-one, he said, "No drinks for her." she appreciated his protectiveness, realizing that no matter where she was, that spirit of protection would always follow her to tell her when she was venturing into the wrong lane. "You can play pool," he said, "but I am not giving you a drink."

People often said to her, "You have that face that says you do not belong," in clubs and bars. When she hung out with her sister and her friends sometimes back in the early 1970s, they would ditch her. They ditched her one night, which turned out to be the last time she went out with them. After they came back to the house the next day, they did not speak about it. her sister's conscience was bothering her she finally said, "How did you get to the house?"

she told her this gentleman offered her a ride. He said he had been watching her, and it seems her group had long been gone. He got up from his corner and came over and asked why was she still at the club. she explained that she was waiting on her sister and her friends. He said, "Come on, I will give you a ride and take you home." He wanted to make sure she got home safely. After some nervous debate with him, she accepted his offer. she had heard so many bad things about guys taking girls home that she wasn't sure if she should trust him. But he genuinely sounded more concerned for her safety than trying to make a pass at her.

When he pulled onto her street, she wondered if she should ditch him and run from the car. He caught her attention and unknowingly addressed her indecision. "Which one of these apartments do you live in?" she pointed to the correct entrance, which led to her apartment. He said,

"I would like to walk you to your door." she was startled by his request and quickly said no. He said, "I will sit here until you go in and lock the door behind you. Do not come back out, and don't come to the club with your sister and her friends; that is not a place for you." she said thanks for the ride and for the advice. As she left his car, she promised him she would not hang out with Karen and her friends ever again.

Karen did not return until the second afternoon. Then she remembered him saying, "Your sister and her friends won't be returning home for a couple of days." she wondered how he could know so much about them and where they had gone. Karen walked in with fresh ideas that she stayed away from.

Karen lived in Las Vegas for several years. Connecticut had intolerable winters, for Karen, the changing of the climate made it difficult for her to maneuver with her sickle cell. The changes frequently made her ill, and she decided to move herself and her young daughter to Las Vegas. The weather was more tolerable for Karen in the 1970s, not as wide a range in temperature as Connecticut. Charlotte and her children had stayed in Connecticut.

Then as the days turned into weeks and the weeks turned into months, she would call her sister and check on her and her niece. Karen had found work in a hospital and had long hours. She was dating, and her daughter would stay with friends until she got home from work. This arrangement was not always soundproof, and at times she could hear the voice of her niece calling her name. she was not sure what to make of this voice, so she took it to the Lord. He told her she would have to travel to Las Vegas and get her niece, but in the meanwhile her little voice was calling, "Aunty Chara!" she could not stand to know she needed me to come and help her, so she went to God again and asked Him what she should do. He said make an arrangement to fly to Las Vegas. Charlotte did not have enough money to make the trip and did not have anyone to ask for the money, yet she obeyed His voice got on the phone and made the reservation she continued to work believing she was going to pick up her niece the following weekend, without a doubt reservation was made as the days got close thoughts of doubt tried to creep in, but she believe she was going to get her niece.

One day she was home, and there was a knock at the door. she opened the door to see a man standing there asking her if he could come in and talk with her. she reluctantly let him in and gave him a seat at the dining room table, not far from the front door. As he sat down he tossed a roll of money across the table in her direction. she was not thinking of the trip to Las Vegas, and no one knew about the trip or her lack of finances—no one but God and herself. she was interested in what the stranger had to say. As she put her hands on the money to toss it back across the table to him, the voice of the Lord said, "This is the money I provided for you to make the trip." she put her hand to her mouth and did not know what to say. she asked about his household and the need they might have, but he assured her he was fine and she should accept the money. Then she said, "There is a trip planned but no transportation to get to the airport." She finally said thank you and he got up and left as he came, then he turned and said you will hear from me tomorrow, He promise he would get intouch with charlotte by tomorrow, apparently he knew her schedule, he was back after hearing a knock on the door and she went to open it he was true to his word he gave her a number and she had reservation to get back and forth from the airport.

a shuttle was arranged to and from the airport, she flew to Vegas, and Karen was very glad to see her sister and her little niece. She had to work the next day, so charlotte hung out with her niece and the babysitter and they went to all the places they would go in a day. This was quietly not a good sight, and she explained to her sister that night. She agreed and helped her daughter pack. they left for the airport, the next day heading to Connecticut, her niece and herself.

Karen stayed in Las Vegas for a couple of years before deciding to make her change back to Connecticut. She had a life and took action to make it a reality. It was as thou she crept in to Connecticut, chatlotte cannot remember her sister arrival to Connecticut she crept in quietly and quietly crept out She did not live with her sister before finding her footing, and charlotte had not seen their mom, her mom did not like her having such a close relationship with the Lord, this kept them from having a close relationship. she did not keep in touch, so she could not verify whether Karen stayed with her mom or with whom she stayed with. The whereabouts of Karen, after she had moved back east, to charlottes' mind, was as if she were living in a far away country and could not be reached.

Then one day Karen arrived at charlotte apartment with a little boy sitting on her lap and a huge stomach saying she was pregnant with twins. she was ecstatic for her and her new family; the doctors had told her she could not have children because of her sickle cell disease. There they were: the oldest child did not have the disease, her oldest son had the disease, but the twins did not have the disease. She was blessed, and she was thankful about having her family.

Karen had conquered more than her share of her life she had a husband and her children which allowed her to beat all odds. Charlotte began encouraging her to find a church where she felt comfortable and don't mind saying she attend pastor so and so church charlotte liked the church Karen had chosen to attend he have a lot of tent services and traveled to New York often to hold tent services. She did that also. She did not want to attend the same church her sister was attending; that was fine with charlotte "Just find a church you are comfortable in." She really liked the church where Karen settled in; her pastor was newly married they had very young children, they held a lot of tent services, outside on their church property as well as in and around their own city while traveling from city to city or outdoors. People enjoy tent services and many people would attend a tent service visiting from other churches. charlotte would attend many of the services with Karen. she would always bring in the New Year at church, and Karen and her children would always attend these services with her and charlotte children.

When the Lord separated charlotte from Karen, she made arrangements that were comfortable for her and accepted an offer from her cousin instead of keeping the traditional pattern to go and spend New Year's giving thanks to the Lord. Her cousin, a friend, and their sisters decided to ring in the New Year at a club in New York.

Karen called charlotte to talk about her arrangement and her entourage—and about a disagreement the group were having, she explained to Karen that she should take the group to a New Year's church service. She said if you come to Connecticut plans would change and we would go to church this was too short a notice to travel east, the arrangement could be changed and a different plan could be made. She felt the rejection in her spirit and knew she could not disobey the Lord and try to make the trip. she was on schedule that night and nightly for the rest of the week at the hospital; there was no canceling of work. she had bills and children who depended on her income. she could not consider the request on such short notice.

It was December 31 when the phone rang. It was already a difficult night; we were moving gurneys from the third floor to the basement in shifts. As one patient went up, someone was coming down with a gurney. Our energy had been spent. The cloud on the floor was dark that night; even the light from the ceiling didn't seem to give its full power. Then the hospital receptionist put through a call to charlotte, there was a emergency from a doctor in Connecticut, saying the doctor wanted to speak to Karen's next of kin. Before Karen was unable to speak, she made sure to tell the doctor to call and ask for charlotte and confide in her. Walking to the phone her knees got a little weak and she had full reception of the hospital in Connecticut she had knowledge.

He told her Karen had passed away, she was bleeding from every pore, and there was nothing he could do to save her. The sickle cell had made it difficult for him to excel in treatment. She had come to the Emergency department after a party, where the alcohol had triggered her sickle cell. Karen had called charlotte when she came in from the club and said she had gotten sick from the club and had left. The moment she left the club and got home she called charlotte to say she had drunk a Guinness stout and begun feeling pain.it was all gibberish clear English could not be heard that knowledge she was not to hear. Everyone had come home with her. Someone made her a cup of tea and said they used the cup of sugar that was on the counter. After she drank the tea, she began having cramps. She said they were now waiting on an ambulance. Then shortly the doctor called, and no one knew where the cup of sugar had come from or where it disappeared to.

Yet charlotte asked the doctor about an autopsy, but he said it would not be necessary to have one. For two weeks Karen's body sat in the funeral home freezer. The mortician had begun calling, but there was no release in her spirit to make the trip to Connecticut. as he asked her how he should present the body as naturally as possible. she said she was Caucasian, but the mortician said, "She is not Caucasian; her body is black." Then he said, "In my twenty-five years' experience, when a body comes in different from its usual color, this might be from arsenic poisoning."

"Arsenic?" was charlotte instant response. "Where would anyone get that?" He said from a hospital medicine cabinet, where medical personnel have access to the key. It was as if that was the information the Lord wanted me to have. charlotte then felt release in her spirit, and over the next two days arrangements were made, and there was a funeral. she always remembered the sermon story of a goat that had fell in a deep ditch and dug around the edges of the hole until enough dirt was packed underfoot for him to jump from the hole. But just as she had the vision from God about the club and the opened bottles left on the table, so God had provided her with the details of her sister's every moment until the ambulance came. Charlotte always questioned God about why He would allow certain things to happen. For example, why go into a certain generation and have the elders and their young ones killed? Then He would explain. Most times He literally showed charlotte why these things must be uprooted. The evil would rise up in the third and fourth generation. But if there is true repentance and the seed is eradicated through the blood of Jesus, then that person's life will be saved. This brings to mind the story of Mephibosheth; he was five years old when he was accidently injured as his nurse was trying to protect him from the upheaval of soldiers trying to destroy the lineage of Saul. He was the son of Jonathan and grandson of Saul, who took his own life when he heard his son had been killed. It was customary that when a ruler had been killed, there would be no claimant to the throne, the family would be killed also.

To think that God had brought Karen and charlotte to America, where they could have sufficient food to eat, increased education, and jobs for income. But instead of praising Him, Karen chose to give praise to the adversary. This was more than she could accept. she came to realize that God is not a Sunday morning person but the powerful Savior of our souls, active in every detail of our daily lives; and that the only thing required of us is simple faith and obedience, believing that He is the almighty Father God and that His Son, Jesus, is Lord and Savior. God cares about our daily survival and desires to be more than our provider; He desires that we be in intimate relationship with Him. We need to develop that relationship with God, in the name of Jesus.

In spirit, she had seen in advance the circumstances Karen had put herself in, and she had been unable to divert her intention. she had tried to warn Karen over the phone, before Karen went out that night—just as she had always warned Karen about her lifestyle, but it was as if only gibberish came out of charlotte mouth, as if she had a dumb spirit, sounding as a dumb person without words. her inability to speak audible to Karen about the vision she had seen brought her to understand why Zechariah could not utter a word about naming his son until after the son's birth. God had made the decision and it was out of Zechariah's hands. His son was to be named John, which means "Yahweh is gracious."

she had gained a greater understanding that God's ways are not our ways; His thoughts are higher. she could only trust blindly that God no longer wanted Karen to have human intervention or interpretation. He had sealed my tongue from uttering a word of caution for that particular night. His Son's name had been rejected, and God's divine decision was made to also reject any further guidance for Karen.

We must give God praise and thanks every moment of our lives, for He is the almighty God who knows all and grants every person the freedom to accept Jesus as Savior-or not. It was in writing the eight chapter that charlotte faith was unveiled, and she realized that she operate under the unadulterated faith in which God wants us to operate. she then realized she solely trusted and depended on Jesus for victory in a matter she could not control.

Isaiah 26:3–4 (KJV) says, "Thou wilt keep him in perfect peace, whose mind is stayed on thee: because he trusteth in thee. Trust ye in the Lord forever: for in the Lord Jehovah is everlasting strength." The feeling that overwhelmed charlotte now was the same anointing as on the day of Pentecost when the Holy Ghost came in the hotel room and filled her with His sweet, sweet anointing. Now, as she reflected, she realized that the same anointing had been poured out on her again, and even as she sat there, trying to fit in that presence, it wouldn't come upon her. she believe that anointing was coming from a place that human power simply cannot access; it has to come from a divine presence.

Psalm 125:1–2 (KJV) says, "They that trust in the Lord shall be as mount Zion, which cannot be removed, but abideth forever. As the mountains are round about Jerusalem, so the Lord is round about his people from henceforth even forever."

CHAPTER 8

Black or White?

In Karen's eyes, she had evolved into a woman of determination and poise, who lived as though she were white. At times in America's history, there was still a great prejudice distinction between white and black workin class women. It was far more common to see black women in labor jobs like domestic work than in office jobs, but when charlotte came to the United States, she realized that white people thought of themselves as superior, and she felt that they had not earned the privilege to believe themselves greater than her.

she knew what hunger was. Although she had been hungry once in her life, that was an experience she felt she was able to tell the world about: not knowing where the next meal was coming from or how far you had to walk to get the food or how soon after you got there you could eat something. She felt privileged and went after the jobs that she liked and did not let what people said about domestic, blue collar, or white collar jobs interfere with what she wanted.

Karen understood clearly that people of color would have a difficult time getting into certain jobs; this was not charlotte concern. her first concern was to understand the behavior of white people and realize that they depended on us as we depended on them; we were not separate from each other. Our thinking about ourselves and the stories of our forefathers has brought such a veil over us that we are not able to rise.

No woman likes competition, and a man only uses what his sister, his mother, or his wife says about his ability to provide for his family as a reason to degrade and destabilize competitors. Rhetoric and economic rulership will always offset a nation. There are no competitions in disaster; every man's hand is to the plow, and whether you knew him before, you know of him now. His name is Jesus. People have capitulated to the demands of the forces of the air; they have lost their hope in God.

One morning as charlotte was leaving the house for work, she walked down the path toward the street when a calling voice behind her called, "Hey, come here." she had not passed anyone on her way from the building, so she turned to learn who could be calling. she saw a woman's head protruding out of the ground. charlotte stood for a moment staring at the head, and then the woman said, "Come here." She beckoned with a finger for her to come towards her. she walked over to the woman, who said, "Come down here," looking down into an opening. she could see there was life down there. she began walking down steps that led into the underground. she followed the woman as she went back to her desk. She asked charlotte, "Who are you?"

Her question caught me off guard, and she gave her a puzzled look. "Why are you asking me this?"

The woman answered, "Are you black or are you white?"

"My father is black; my mother is black." Then a screen appeared and she saw her sister. "That's my sister," sheI said; "she is white."

"But who are you?" she asked again.

"Why are you asking me this?" charlotte was still confused over the point the woman was trying to make.

"We can see who your sister is, but though your skin is black, you act white,-you talk white, and you dress white."

God was leading her through this experience. she had not considered the difference in character between her and her sister and still could not make contact with it because it was who she was, and she was not trying to live anyone else's life.

She believe God wanted her to know that others see the choices we each make in our lives, that we and others are impacted by those choices, which are either darkness or light, and that skin color should have no bearing on our choices. Black or white, He sees all and loves all and desires a relationship of light with us, and He desires that we make choices that lead us closer to the light of His Spirit rather than to despair and destruction.

her thoughts took her back to childhood how she had not wanted Karen to feel badly that she didn't know her dad. she thought it must have been at that time that Karen changed inside, adopting the identity of a black woman and the lifestyle that came with it. her own personality change, to that of a white woman, although she had no example of what a white woman should do or how she lived. The accepting of her name, Charlotte rather than Joan, also played a great role in the character of who she was to become.

Karen with her light skin had adopted an African American lifestyle, while charlotte with her dark skin had adopted a Caucasian lifestyle. Several people both black and white had asked the same question: "Why does she speak so differently? She is natural, and she is herself." she could not vision the separation of whom people were looking at or talking about. she could not give priority to their question; she could only be herself as she am. she never gave priority to their questions. she was preoccupied with her struggles as a black woman working in a white woman's world. It was not a struggle for her to maintain her posture as herself because she never looked at white people as better than her because she saw them in other settings and was culture shocked; therefore she knew they had their struggles, and yes, she had hers'.

she would walk down the street and see and know what others didn't about racial assumptions and expectations. Yet she would smile and shake hands as if her existence wasn't cluttered with questions and confusion with her feet planted in two different worlds. her inner spirit was in turmoil and starving. At that time she didn't have the knowledge to feed herself with the Spirit of God and His living Word. her life had taken a whirlwind turn, which drove her thoughts away from God and church. But because her life was not her own, there was always a soft still voice that would slip in, and she could hear herself saying the Lord's Prayer. Then that little unction would revive her mind to seek closer guidance if she yielded to the calling for a closer walk, because "He walks with me and He talks with me, and he tells me I am His own." And the voice I hear as I tarry there is none other than the Lord's.

CHAPTER 9

True to God and True to Yourself

When charlotte was a child about five years old, her dad had insisted that her Mom dress her up for church every Sunday and make sure she goes into the church. Of all the siblings in her mom's house, she was the only one who went to church. Mom never let her miss a Sunday mass, and she developed a relationship with "a voice" that talked with her and walked with her. It was not until she was grown and more spiritually mature that she understood that the "voice" was the Spirit of God within her.

Several years after she had moved to Connecticut as a young adult moving from German town, the Lord had one of Karen's churchgoing friends paula to approach her and ask if she would be willing to participate in a two-day fast. she asked the woman when the fast would begin. The woman responded, "Starting this evening."

she replied, "Starting this afternoon? I just took out what I plan to prepare for dinner." Now she was being asked to cook for her family but not to eat any of it for two days.

"Yes" was her reply. she thought the woman had lost her mind, asking her to give up meals for two days. she went over the menu with paula trying to mentally focus on the question she had asked her. "Jamaican style rice and beans, steak, fried plantain and carrot juice to wash it down."

paula, being Jamaican herself, licked her lips and said, "You can still prepare the meal. Just refrain from eating any of it until the fast is over."

charlotte thought about what she would be giving up for a fast and how-to take her thoughts off the things of the world, which can captivate us to such distraction, we eventually get deeper, believing we can fix something in a world that is not our home. charlotte wanted this commitment with the Lord and a closer walk with Him, who had been there throughout the years when she did not know of Him except as "the voice." she responded that she wanted to fast if paula would fast with her. She agreed to fast with Charlotte, and Charlotte turned her plate over and fasted unto the Lord. As she walked away from the presence of the woman, paula laughed and said, "It is only your beginning." And that was indeed the beginning for charlotte. When she checked on paula, she did not keep her promise to fast, but charlotte was grateful that God had used paula to intervene in her downward walk to nowhere, looking for hope in a place where there could be no peace. This is a place of preparation, to be ready to go back with God when He comes in a moment, in the twinkling of an eye. We can get caught up in the tares, but when He comes, we have to be willing and ready to say, "Yes, Father, here I am," and turn back unto him.

charlotte went home and cooked the meal, which she could not taste while it was cooking or eat after it was prepared. Two days after the hour she had committed to fast and pray, she ate the meal, and the flavor was right. she started going to church with paula and recalled a childhood experience when she had inadvertently entered into the hand-clapping, tambourine-beating, drum-thumping music of a church service just like the one shes' now being a member of, while playing in the woods with her friends and cousins. We were playing catch, tapping each other and then running wildly, trying to get away from being caught. she heard music nearby and was drawn by the rhythm into a makeshift building where the women were wearing long white dresses, singing and clapping their hands, and playing instruments …. she immediately felt welcome among them, her cousins and friends try to convince her not to enter through the door but the spirit said go and in she went to the music she love to dance and dance she did until one of the mothers put her arm around her shoulder and said where is your mother, she told her they were visiting from town, and her mom was with her sisters, well the mother said go home and don't come back until your mom come with you, she felt disappointed to hear those words, she knew her mom would not bring her, she left the building, but her heart never left what she felt that day, her memory came flooding in, that memory she carried with her until when she walked into that church with her sisters' friend paula, there no one told her to, "Go home, and don't return unless your mother brings you."

With that memory came a greater understanding about the difference in dance rhythm with the unity of the body of Christ-sharing worship and praise to God, sharing prayer and fasting, and feeding together on the Word of God week after week. The pastor talked about the Holy Ghost and said that in order to profess you have the Holy Ghost, you should have the evidence of speaking in another tongue. she made the gift of tongues her petition, along with the other young people in the church. We would gather every Tuesday night at the altar, get on our knees and call on the name of Jesus. she felt herself going deeper into His presence.

As she continued her call to Jesus, a bright light shone around her, and then an image of a cross appeared. she saw the cross standing planted on a small mound of dirt, leaning to one side, so low that its arm almost touched the ground. The cross-looked worn, tattered, and extremely tired. she did not know what to think; she just kept looking at it. Then she jumped to her feet, and as she stood up, her pastor was standing behind her. she did not hear the pastor when she left the pulpit; she only knew her hand was on her shoulders, coaxing her back onto her knees. charlotte tried explaining to the pastor that something was there, but the pastor said, "Don't lose the vision; get back on your knees."

she did and found the cross was still there. she began taking a closer look at the cross; it looked so rugged. It was stained with tears, pain, and suffering. When she tried standing again, she couldn't. she heard a voice that sounded as though it was saying something to her, but she could not hear what it said. It sounded like "Carry the cross," but it was not clear enough for her to understand. she tried standing again but couldn't, so she began talking to God, telling Him she could not stand because there was a weight on her back. she tried standing again; this time she came up, but her knees were bent. she got back on her knees and said I still could not stand. Then when she tried standing yet again, she was able to stand. she still felt the pressure as if she was carrying a weight, but she was able to stand.

Although she had seen the vision of the cross and the light shining around her as it shone around Saul on his way to Damascus, she had not yet received the gift of speaking a spiritual language.

The following Sunday, her church had a visiting pastor. When he was finish preaching he called a prayer line, she went to the altar for prayer and attempted again to speak in a spiritual tongue but without clear success. The pastor told her that she had experienced only a touch or a sprinkling of the anointing of the Holy Ghost. The pastor was right but her desire was to speak the language full and audible unto the Lord. After the revival she continued to tarry at the altar to be filled by the Holy Ghost with the gift of tongues, others were praying. But the anointing of tongues did not come to her. It was the month of convocation where the churches gather to give their report and different ones preach, three set of family traveled to Greensville N.C.

The pastor, charlotte and her two children, another evangelis the mother of the church and her family.

One of the evangelists that rode with charlotte to share the driving also shared a room at the motel with her and her children. We had gotten freshen up and headed to the church the spirit was in operation and service was in session after her and her children had gotten to the service after driving all night she stayed at church for awhile then left the service ahead of the evangelist to get her children in bed. They had been up and needed to rest. After she said prayers with her children, they were sound asleep at once. After The evangelist came in and got ready for bed; she got on her knees and began praying. Charlotte rolled out of bed and began praying with her.

A few seconds into prayer, charlotte began speaking in the ultimate indescribable language she had hoped for. It was supreme! Then after a few words in the supreme language, another tongue came from her mouth. Since that night she have carried the anointing of tongues, but not the supreme tongue she first experienced.

While she experienced the bright light shining around her and seeing the old rugged cross only once, there have been other instances when a light would shine inside her body that she could see, whether her eyes were closed or open. The light lets her know God is examining her life, and that makes her feel closer to God. she then understood that the light is the presence of God that shines brightly when one has God's attention through prayer and worship. The light of God's presence, like the gift of tongues, is a way in which He lets her know that she's in His presence.

she could not walk away from who she truly was deep inside, so she continued to consistently encourage herself with reminders that her true identity did not rest in the fact that she was a mother or a nursing assistant. she had come to know that her true identity was rooted in Jesus Christ—that she was righteousness in the eyes of God and that she was His daughter. she reminded herself that God had placed her on earth to complete a divinely appointed mission and that her life was not her own but devoted in service to God. she also remembered that she was never alone; the Spirit of God was always with her. But she still struggled to see clearly his purpose beyond serving faithfully as a mother, raising her children in the ways of the Lord, and working as a nursing assistant who reached beyond her duties and truly cared for others as God cares for her.

Serving as a good Samaritan is what God requires of us, but that service to others was co-opted long ago by the world—those who do not call Jesus Lord. Although nursing is a legal profession, it is also a mercenary gift to the vulnerable. As she give, we should give God all the glory for every gift because every good thing comes from God, no matter how little or large.

> Every good and perfect gift is from above, coming
> down from the Father of the heavenly lights, who does
> not change like shifting shadows. (James 1:17)

At times she would see glimpses of the broader picture for her life, but she could not bring those glimpses into clear focus. When she would attempt to write about those glimpses, the words would melt away, but the vision remained, although vague, as if she were attempting to embrace a cloud. But she believed by faith that God had everything in her life and in her sphere of influence in His divine control—even in the years she spent with her beloved sister Karen. she continued to work diligently as a mother and as a nursing assistant, trusting that her positions in life were indeed aligned with God's complete purpose for her.

CHAPTER 10

Who Are You?

If someone were to ask you, "Who are you?" would you be able to stand tall and confident and share that you are a princess, the adopted daughter or son of the king of kings, the most high God, your Creator? Would you be able to share that you are rooted and grounded in faith as a believer in Jesus Christ? Would you be able with confidence to say that you know who God created you to be and for what purpose? Would you be able to list the spiritual and natural gifts with which He has blessed you?

Most important, would you be confident in sharing with absolute certainty that you know where you will be when you take your last breath and where you will spend all of eternity?

It does not matter the color of your skin, where you were born, whom you know, how well or badly you have behaved, or what others think of you. The only true things that count in this earthly life are how God-in His great love, mercy, and forgiveness sees you and how you see yourself in His revealing light: as His princess or a prince, an heir to His throne if you have accepted His Son, Jesus, as your personal Savior.

It only matters that you have stepped out in faith, believing that wherever the winds have taken you, God will find you needing Him and His divine direction. It only matters that what you have heard from the beginning will take root, and when you stumble upon water you will not refuse to drink of that living water and be refreshed.

We were given to our parents from the premortal world, married or single. We were placed in the womb of the woman with an earthly father being the recipient. We were brought up to believe we go to preschool, kindergarten, junior high school, high school, and then college. We then ventured into the world to find a job and a spouse and begin the process all over again, each of us with parenting skills different from those of our parents. But that only sums up the basics to life. Or does it?

We have intervention and networking with others that does not reveal its full potential. That is why we struggle, Looking through a glass darkly. A scripture that would likely bring us closer to the real basics of life states the pattern that we should apprehend and expound as children of God working out our soul salvation in order to return with him. But the diabolical misgivings were so overwhelming that we gravitated to its drift.

> But their minds were blinded. For until this day the same veil remains unlifted in the reading of the Old Testament, because the veil is taken away in Christ. But even to this day, when Moses is read, a veil lies on their heart. Nevertheless when one turns to the Lord, the veil is taken away. Now the Lord is the Spirit; and where the Spirit of the Lord is, there is liberty. (2 Corinthians 3:14–17 NKJV)

The world is not our home.

Isaiah 44:18 (NKJV) says, "They do not know nor understand; for He has shut their eyes, so that they cannot see, and their hearts, so that they cannot understand." And so that we do not contaminate the things of God with those of the world, we cannot see clearly the motion of God's purpose because of the veil that He uses to cover every section of His purpose.

Second Corinthians 3:16 says that when you turn to the Lord, the veil is taken away, and as the veil is being removed, you can see that there are other things hidden also behind other veils, which will not be revealed until God believes we are ready for His revelations. The veil is like a sheet, a huge white covering that allows no transparency, and you only get a glimpse of what is to come.

charlotte had moved into this neighborhood, but her box spring was still lying on the floor. The sun was unbearable hot and the swamp cooler was giving into the rays of the sun she was miserable the unbearably heat, and the swamp cooler was no matched to the rays of the sun. she was miserable. The neighbor said the swamp cooler needed water. she did not know anything about swamp coolers or air conditioning; just turn on the switch for them to operate. Overwhelmed, she layed down on the coverings over the box spring. she felt heavy and sleepy, but as she lay on the box spring, between sleep and wake she began to see movement and action. she fought off the heaviness of sleep she had to stay awake.

Just a few feet from her there was an opening as if a sheet like curtain had been drawn open, and these little people—as we call them in our storybooks elves—appeared. They were making something. she lay still, watching them constructing a building made with words. The alphabet they used fastened together without hammer or nails; it simply fit. she was shocked to see their construction, but she lay so still that her blood needed circulation, so she moved her body a little. This movement made them aware that someone was watching them They looked toward the opening, but she lay still again, even holding her breath and breathing in whispers. They did not want to be observed.

Then in the box spring she heard something like rats squealing and playing as if basketball. she did not move as long as they did not run across her. she wanted to see this vision at all costs. They heightened their security and were more attentive to my presence. They had drawn the curtains a little, but they continued to work. They were making decisions and holding meetings as to their next move for installing another alphabet, pointing to the next area to be fastened. The rats had my attention; they sounded as though they had a good game of basketball going. Then the little breaths became a deep breath, and someone said, "We should close this." They made the decision to close the curtain, and in a swift moment it was drawn closed. The basketball game stopped. she got up and went to the living room. The heaviness had left, and she lay on the couch and turned on the television thinking about what she just saw and how the rats were suppose to scare her away from the vision. she looked around the room and saw a rat, red in color, sitting, not hiding, watching TV with her. She moved her body by reaching for something on the coffee table but he was unmovable, not caring to be under cover, watching the television. she began watching the TV. After a while she turned her head; he was still there. Then she fell asleep, and when she woke, he was gone. He returned two other nights to watch TV then he never came again.

> For we know that if our earthly house, this tent, is destroyed, we have a building from God, a house not made with hands, eternal in the heavens. For in this we groan, earnestly desiring to be clothed with our habitation which is from heaven, if indeed, having been clothed, we shall not be found naked. For we who are in this tent groan, being burdened, not because we want to be unclothed, but further clothed, that mortality may be swallowed up by life. Now He who has prepared us for this very thing is God, who also has given us the Spirit as a guarantee. (2 Corinthians 5:1–5 NKJV)

My Father, My Father, I look for my father. My father carried me in the clavicle of His neck; His collarbone was my pillow, I look for my Father in the crowd, I look for my Father in the cloud, I look for you.

My Father, My Father, my Father is here. I snuggle in the neck of my Father, I raise my head and look up in the face of my Father, which is a block of cloud. The voice of my Father soothes me, and I rest.

Yet He is not. I no longer rest in the clavicle of my Father; I no longer look up in the face of a block of cloud. I cry and cry. It is a strange place; my mind is temporarily at rest. There are many people—a mother and a father, a father who adores her and a mother who is distant unless Father is present.

My Father hears, though He hears not. My Father sees, though He sees not.

If only I could picture yesterday, I would see you there. I look at you … where are you?

I reach out my hands, and the winds reach through my fingers.

My Father, My Father. I touch your flesh. You look at me, but corruption rebels. You look past me, as the wind passes through my fingers. I opened my hands, and you turned away like the wind, without a thought.

Where is my Father?

You are not your own; you were bought at a price (see 1 Corinthians 6:19–20).

> Therefore Jesus also, that he might sanctify the people with His own blood, suffered outside the gate. Therefore let us go forth to Him, outside the camp, bearing His reproach. For here we have no continuing city, but we seek the one to come. Therefore by Him let us continually offer the sacrifice of praise to God, that is, the fruit of our lips, giving thanks to His name. But do not forget to do good and to share, for with such sacrifices God is well pleased. (Hebrews 13:12–16 NKJV)

> Then Paul stood in the midst of the Areopagus and said, "Men of Athens, I perceive that in all things you are very religious; for as I was passing through and considering the objects of your worship, I even found an altar with the inscription:

> TO THE UNKNOWN GOD

> Therefore, the One whom you worship without knowing, Him I proclaim to you: God, who made the world and everything in it, since He is Lord of heaven and earth, does not dwell in temples made with hands. Nor is He worshiped with men's hands, as though He needed anything, since He gives to all life, breath, and all things. And He has made from one blood every nation of men to dwell on all the face of the earth, and has determined their preappointed times and the boundaries of their dwellings, so that they should seek the Lord, in the hope that they might grope for Him and find Him, though He is not far from each one of us … (Acts 17:22–27 NKJV)

When a vision is captured, a leader is designed. When God saw the vision, He designed Jesus Christ.

God saw that man and woman and children would need to be reconnected back to Him because their innocence was invaded, and got disconnected from Him. When Eve's eyes were opened, and God realized that from the womb the blood could not be common, sharing between mother and child, not only would the blood not be common, but God designed His vision so that the one who accepts His vision would be considered married, and the Spirit of God will dwell in the belly of man. Therefore you are no longer common, and are to live a life as a wife, whose husband is God. As the womb of a woman carries a child, yet the blood of the mother is separate from the child, so God has designed His vision so you can have a physical husband. Yet he is your spiritual husband; therefore you have to live a sanctified life and a holy life unto God and to your physical husband. You have the vision of God.

Printed in the United States
By Bookmasters